Recovering a Sense of the Sacred

Conversations with Thomas Berry

A Memoir By

Carolyn W. Toben

Timberlake Earth Sanctuary Press

2012

Published by
Timberlake Earth Sanctuary Press
1501 Rock Creek Dairy Road
Whitsett, NC 27377
www.timberlakeearthsanctuary.com

Edited by Scott H. Davis

Cover Art by Mary Southard, CSJ
"For A New Birth"
Copyright © 2009 by Mary Southard, CSJ
www.MarySouthardArt.org

Thomas Berry Photograph by Lou Niznik

ISBN 978-0-9883928-0-9

For my beloved nine grandchildren and for
all children with the prayer that they might find
the inner presence of Love that binds all
creatures, humans, trees, plants, sun, moon
and stars into one sacred earth community.

Thomas Berry

Contents

Foreword

An Intimate Communion of Thought

From the foothills of the world's oldest mountain chain, the Southern Appalachians, and in the tradition of such spiritual classics as Gurdjieff's *Meetings With Remarkable Men,* comes Carolyn Toben's *Recovering a Sense of the Sacred* at a time that is not only propitious, but providential.

Maybe once every hundred years someone emerges from the shuddering mass of humanity who speaks to us with a kind of clarity and wisdom that is universally profound. Father Thomas Berry is such a figure. He was born and raised in a lush and verdant part of the country where nature and beauty trumped progress and development. In this place and in a special meadow near his boyhood home, the seeds of a universal vision for the earth and humanity were cultivated and nurtured—seeds, which grew eventually to become a vision that is biblical in its insights, wisdom and compassion.

We know from our literary canons and our mythologies of the meeting of great minds. But what about the meeting of great souls? Western spirituality and philosophy have not documented many, if any, of these kinds of conversations. But, here, in the North Carolina hill country, a meeting took place and an in-depth conversation was born—lasting more than a decade—that has produced a document that may be as profoundly and dynamically consciousness-raising as it is rare.

In the tradition of the call-and-response of the old Southern African-American spirituals, we find in these pages a call-and-response between a man and a woman who have given over their lives to "the greater good." This conversation and this book couldn't have come at a more critical time in the human-earth drama, when the lack of our ability to see things *wholistically* has brought human civilization to the brink of its own demise. In times like these, new metaphors, new ideas, new commitments need to be made in order to bridge the necessary transition to a more harmonious and sustainable future.

But this is not a book filled with gloom and doom. In fact, it is the opposite. This conversation between Thomas Berry and Carolyn Toben *is* that bridge many of us have been looking for in the world and within ourselves. With her questions and personal responses born of a lifetime of teaching and of spiritual seeking and practice, Carolyn Toben not only provides one of the great sages of our century a divine platform from which to speak to humanity at this most precious and precipitous of historic moments, but then adds her own distilled and intimate reflections to further ferment, sweeten and make palatable Thomas Berry's "wine."

So richly simple are Thomas Berry's responses to Carolyn's calling out for much-needed wisdom, that any young person can intuitively grasp and understand them In fact, Thomas reaches out here, specifically, to children and young adults, and he addresses the years ahead that they will be facing and what their mission will be. Hence, the genius of this book, which is a manual for interdependence, transformation and communion. In reading these pages one finds oneself singing "the hymn of praise that is existence," as Thomas Berry called it. In singing this inner song, we are wed to what is sacred in our lives—and with gratitude, are finally home.

I knew Thomas Berry for the last twenty years of his life and met Carolyn Toben about the same time that I met him. The two of them walked parallel paths, which kept synchronistically crossing my own. At those intersections, we shared "an intimate communion of thought,' as Thomas would have said. And it was just this kind of communion that led Carolyn to humbly write, "Let the universe in all its marvelous differentiation teach me to celebrate differences in all the relationships of my life." This focus on diversity within unity and this kind of sacred context are exactly at the heart of Thomas Berry's message for the ages, leading us, as he himself did over the course of his own lifetime, to continually seek and to increasingly *see*. His ideas (which are expanded in his books, *The Dream of the Earth, The Great Work* and *The Universe Story),* here distilled, are now accessible and available to us all. This is "required reading" for our time. I firmly believe that those who have read this book will be forever changed.

Thomas Rain Crowe
Author of *Zoro's Field: My Life in the Appalachian Woods*
Tuckasegee, North Carolina
September 2012

Introduction

My Great Companion

This is a story of transformation ... of ourselves and of the earth, for the two are inextricably interwoven. Thus it is a story of relationships, both in the largest sense and in an individual sense. It is a story of how all living forms of earth might recover life-giving relationships with each other in a time of perilous transition on our planet. It is a story of the struggle to recover a relationship with the earth, the universe and the soul through a sense of the sacred. It is a love story of learning to see through the eyes of the heart.

It is also a personal story of my relationship with a man who was called a monk, a scholar, a priest, a mystic, a cultural historian, a shaman, a storyteller and more. In his lifetime he was the recipient of eight honorary doctoral degrees, the author of nine books, and was honored all over the world for his work in bringing into consciousness a renewed vision of the human-earth relationship.

His lifelong concern for the well-being and survival of the planet was recognized by the United Nations, the Center for Respect of Life and Environment, the Catholic Church, as well as countless organizations, tribes and individuals in many countries and cultures to whom he brought a sustaining presence and new understanding. When he died in 2009, his life was celebrated widely around the world.

The man was Thomas Berry, whom I had the great privilege of knowing as a personal friend and "gracious companion into the twenty-first century," as he once called me in an inscription on a sheaf of poetry. Thomas had many such companions, or "bread fellows," as the word truly means, on a modern day pilgrimage into creating a new century away from the death, destruction and materialism of the twentieth century. These companions came from many walks of life, many wisdom traditions, many ethnic backgrounds. All were seeking a new context for their lives and motivation for human action: new ways of seeing and new transformed ways of being.

They were governmental leaders, religious leaders, economists, scientists, environmentalists, students, missionaries, scholars—a diverse exodus community seeking liberation from limited beliefs in a worldview that has led to humankind's separation from the earth, the universe, the Divine, one another, and from our own souls. To each Thomas Berry was a guide. To each he gave a deeply individualized response. To each he gave a guiding vision away from the cultural pathology of our times. To all he brought a binding-back to one universe in which we are all connected, human and non-human, as a single earth community that lives or dies together.

My Personal Story

I met Thomas Berry for the first time in the winter of 1978. I was teaching a class for adults in Greensboro, North Carolina in which his sister Tess Kelleher was a student. One day after class, Tess came up to me with a gold-colored booklet from a place called the Riverdale Center for Religious Research in New York. "This was written by my brother," she said as she placed it in my hands. "I think you might find it interesting." The book was entitled, *Contemporary Spirituality.*

I took it home and read the manuscript with deep interest. It was an account of the "Old Story," an account of how the world came to be, how we fit into it, how it gave meaning to our lives, and how values were transmitted through it. Thomas Berry wrote with reverence of the story's power to give our lives context, purpose and action, but he also said the story "works in its limited orbit" and was no longer effective at stopping "the dissolution of our institutions and life programs that continue in every phase of our present society."

He went on to write, "We need a *new story* that enlarges the context of our lives and gives us a direction for allowing our lives to function in a meaningful way. We need a new sacred story."

As an educator and parent, I had been carrying these same concerns for many years, recognizing the growing dysfunctional social forms that did not support the inner development of the individual, especially the child. My postgraduate studies had taken me into an exploration of spirituality, world religions and depth psychology for answers, and I felt a glimpse of hopefulness when I read Thomas' words. Impulsively, I picked up the phone and called the Riverdale Center. Thomas answered the phone himself, and when I asked if I might fly up to New York to meet him, his instant response was, "Come ahead."

So on a Monday morning in January 1978, I flew into LaGuardia Airport to have my first experience of the presence of Thomas Berry.

I was accompanied by a former student teacher of mine and we were surprised to see a light snow beginning to fall as the plane landed. As we disembarked from the flight, a slightly built gray-haired gentleman in shirtsleeves came forward calling my name. (I later learned from Thomas' sister that he had given away his coat to someone in a London subway whom he described as a person "needing it more than I did.")

As we proceeded to the airport parking lot to look for his car, I felt an overwhelming appreciation and amazement at his courtesy and kindness in driving all the way to the airport on a snowy morning to meet total strangers. As we drove out of the airport, I realized that my passenger-side window would not roll up all the way and that the windshield wipers were moving rather sluggishly. Yet Thomas was completely undaunted by the circumstances and started down Interstate 398 toward the Riverdale Center in the Bronx. He peered out cautiously between erratic windshield wipes as snow slanted in through my window.

I remember his remarking that he hoped to be "present" for our visit because he had just returned from a weekend with Jacques Cousteau reflecting on the question, "Who owns the seas!"

It was my first direct impression of the depth and breadth of Thomas Berry's intense concern for the whole earth.

Once at the Riverdale Center, Thomas apologetically offered us tea and crackers, the only things he had available, and then began the conversation with "Tell me about yourselves." This, I would come to understand later, was the way he always began to relate to others. So moved by his graciousness, as well as his obvious scholarship, I could only stammer some meager information about my work and how much I appreciated his sister Tess, which he received with obvious pleasure.

I also told him how much the "New Story" meant to me and how deeply concerned I was to work from the new perspective his thinking had offered—how I had been searching all my life for a unified and comprehensive context for the greater understanding it could bring to life.

Thomas listened respectfully with a quality of attention I had never before experienced and then led us into his small publishing room to give us a copy of every one of his monographs to take home. Afterward, he drove us to the subway station and we made our way back to the airport and our return flight to North Carolina.

This was my introduction to a man whose life and work would influence the spiritual and intellectual history of the twentieth and twenty-first centuries and who would also transform my life.

The Years Pass

It was twenty-one years later in 1999 before I was to have time again with Thomas Berry. This time it was in Greensboro where he retired in 1995, coming home to his large extended family and his native North Carolina roots. By then he had expanded his influence as a thinker, writer and lecturer through his years at the Riverdale Center. There he had attracted scholars and others from around the globe who were rethinking their work in the light of his vision of a cosmology that united science and religion into a new understanding of earth and all its inhabitants as a sacred community.

Thomas had allowed himself to suffer the full grief and pain of the rampant destruction of eco-systems, the dangerous changes resulting from global warming, the poisoning of the planet through overuse of chemicals, and the extinction of beloved species. Yet he steadfastly continued to work intellectually and spiritually to find the source of the grave error in the structure of thought that was allowing the savage devastation of the planet.

He challenged every view that separated humans from the natural world. "The future can exist only when we understand the universe as composed of subjects to be communed with, not as objects to be exploited," he said in his introduction to *The Great Work*. "The earth is a single community that lives or dies together," he repeated often.

At the same time, he always sought, as he said to me later, to find a "more universal vision" that would reconcile the empirical findings of science with religion and was larger than both. He was seeking nothing less than to bring into consciousness *a new story* in which the earth was the unifying element for all living forms for all time within one universe.

In addition to the Riverdale Papers, Thomas was a prolific writer who authored several books: *Buddhism, Religions of India, The Dream of the Earth, The Universe Story* with Brian Swimme, *The Great Work: Our Way into the Future,* and *Evening Thoughts: Reflecting on Earth as Sacred Community,* the last two written after he retired. Two more books, *The Sacred Universe: Earth, Spirituality, and Religion in the Twenty-First Century* and *The Christian Future and the Fate of Earth* were published posthumously.

Between 1999 and 2009, I was privileged to spend a good deal of time with Thomas as we lived only thirty minutes apart, he in Greensboro and I in Whitsett, North Carolina, just east of the city. My own work of presenting teacher renewal seminars in North Carolina and California had ended with my husband's diagnosis of cancer and his death in 1999. With his passing, I inherited a legacy of land known as Timberlake Farm Earth Sanctuary, which included woods, meadows, creeks and trails, that my family had loved and protected for thirty-two years.

With my three grown sons off in homes of their own, I was suddenly facing decisions about how to continue to care for the land into an uncertain future. At the same time, I was also dealing with the process of grief and acute loneliness as I began to rebuild my life.

Through mutual friends, Thomas learned of my circumstances, and he called and asked to meet with me. So, on a late August evening at the Green Valley Grill in Greensboro, a setting that would become important in this story, I met Thomas for dinner.

Though I had accepted his invitation with thankfulness, when I drove into the parking lot of the O. Henry Hotel, which adjoined the restaurant, I had some concerns that I might burden Thomas with my emotional state. I remember opening the door of the Grill on that late summer evening with a heavy heart that lifted somewhat with the quiet elegance of the restaurant's high ceilings, dark mahogany booths, and the soft aroma of fresh lilies in an ornate vase on the highly polished table in the foyer.

I was shown to one of the booths where Thomas was already sitting, munching on hard rolls from a basket in front of him. He immediately rose and greeted me warmly with the same deep kindness I remembered from our first meeting. Once we settled in with glasses of wine, he began, as he had done twenty-one years earlier with, "Tell me about yourself."

To my surprise and embarrassment, I blurted out my whole story, including the legacy of land that had been bequeathed to me, and my struggles with grief and loneliness. Thomas listened with his deep quality of special attention and then spoke slowly and gently. "Stay with the grief and it will ultimately heal you. Most people bob right back up to the surface. Blessed are they who can grieve."

He then went on to speak to my expressions of loneliness and lack of a sense of community. "Lack of community, you say? You live in an earth community of woods, meadows, creatures that protect and care for you, as you are caring for them. You live in a *mutually enhancing* relationship with all around you; you need never be lonely."

His words caused something within me to strengthen and uncoil from the dark feelings I had been carrying. I dimly recognized that Thomas Berry was offering me another perspective, another way of "seeing" a new relationship with my home and my land at a very vulnerable time in my life.

I drove home that evening with some tiny new hope for the future. When I arrived home, I took a long walk in the woods with my small dog, Blossom, to begin looking for evidence of a "mutually enhancing relationship" with the land. I didn't know it then, but my conversations and journey with Thomas Berry had just begun.

About This Book

This little book is about my personal conversations with Thomas Berry over a ten-year period, and the inspiration he offered about "a sense of the sacred" for personal and planetary healing.

Through the intervening years, Timberlake Earth Sanctuary became a place where Thomas would come and speak at gatherings about the human-earth relationship, a place where films highlighting his work would be made and shown, a place where he would share meals with earth pilgrims who came from afar to visit him, a place where he even conducted a baptism for one of my grandchildren at our small chapel overlooking Lake Mackintosh.

On several occasions we traveled together to meetings in Asheville and Raleigh, and finally, in the last year of his life, we had a visit every Thursday morning at 10 a.m. at the Wellspring Retirement Community where he died on June 1st, 2009.

Though the circumference of my physical pilgrimage with Thomas was small, the thoughts he shared with me radiated out into a vast universe of ideas where his mind and spirit resided. It was a journey not of miles, but of alchemical moments, of powerful stopping places within the holy temple of his mind that transmuted knowledge into new understanding. If absorbed and understood, these thoughts can bring hope and new direction for our troubled times.

Thomas said, "We are being changed. We are being adjusted to see everything in its proper proportion. We are being driven down to the heart with its radical interior tendencies." And it was through the heart, Thomas suggested, that we could cross the abyss of past consciousness in order to find a new heart-mind connection for our own lives and for the world.

What follows are true stories of moments with Thomas Berry, stopping-places in which he shared with me foundational thoughts that can aid humanity in further stages of evolution. These are large ideas, often repeated throughout the book, which connect us to a vast and sacred universe.

"We are coded," Thomas said, "for the transmission of ideas," and I believe the privilege of receiving these ideas carries with it a responsibility for integrating and sharing them. Therefore in several chapters, I have included my own personal reflections, interpretations, and practices based on my conversations with Thomas.

At the same time, I fully realize that a memoir such as this is limited and partial at best, and that a more comprehensive understanding of Thomas Berry can only be found through a personal study of his extended writings. My hope is that this effort will encourage others to engage in that endeavor.

I once read that our lives are like threads pulling along lasting thoughts, which travel through time that way. Thomas Berry not only pulled along lasting threads through the ages, he wove them together into a new sacred cosmic-human-earth story that brings new vision to this time.

Each reader who receives this vision will have a unique response to the mysterious undertow of possibilities for new life that Thomas' generative perspectives bring forth for our personal lives and our planet. Thomas Berry touched each soul in such a way that it could find its own voice.

My deepest hope for this book is that through Thomas Berry's story, new stories will be inspired and created in word and image and deed, so that the long journey of life might truly become a sacred universal pilgrimage into a new future for the whole earth community.

In deep love and grateful remembrance,
Carolyn Toben
Summer 2012

Chapter One

The Human-Earth Relationship

It was an October day in 1999, a clear blue-sky day in which the air was expectant, promising something special. I had invited fourteen colleagues from my former teacher renewal work at the North Carolina Center for the Advancement of Teaching to gather at Timberlake, the earth sanctuary I inherited following the recent death of my husband, to help me consider the question of what was trying to be born on the land in this historic period. They were from many disciplines in the sciences and the humanities and brought years of experience in working with children and young people. I explained to each of them that I would provide a map of the trails, a bag lunch and time to consider the question.

I also invited Thomas Berry with whom I had renewed my acquaintance at the Green Valley Grill in August. When I called to invite him, he responded with great alacrity, saying: "Oh yes, I'd be delighted."

He arrived that day wearing hard-soled shoes, and I was concerned that at age eighty-four, he might stumble over protruding tree roots on the walking trails, so I suggested that we walk together and he agreed.

We started slowly and silently down the Creeping Cedar Trail, which encircles one of the ponds. I was aware of the stillness of pine trees all around us, birdsong and sun sparkles on the water, as we made our way into the woods. As we reached a large sprawling area of ground cover called creeping cedar, I stopped Thomas and playfully suggested that he close his eyes and open his hands. I picked up a small sprig of the spiraling plant and placed it on his outstretched palms.

Thomas opened his eyes slowly and beheld the tiny plant in his hands, then whispered, "You are so beautiful," and a circuit of love seemed to pass between them that was palpable to witness. In that moment, with the sun shining through the pinewoods on that clear autumn day, I can only say that it seemed that ordinary time stood still, and I felt an enlarged moment in which I could actually feel Thomas Berry's oneness with the earth, the universe, and the Divine.

That fused moment was to live deeply in my memory as a new way of seeing the earth as Thomas Berry saw it, as a "communion of subjects" with everything connected through his vision. It was an opening into a deeper reality in which he and the creeping cedar and the sun and the woods and the universe and the Divine were one. From that moment on, a sense of the unity of all things began a shift in consciousness within me that would evolve through the rest of my life and lead to the birth of a work for children and teachers on the land.

Before our walk was over, I asked Thomas to speak about that special moment of communion. "The human-earth relationship is the primary experience of the Divine," he said slowly. "We are touched by what we touch, we are shaped by what we shape, we are enhanced by what we enhance. The sense of the sacred is at the heart of it all."

His profound words led me to a deep intuitive knowing that my life and work would be forever connected to this moment.

❋ ❋ ❋ ❋ ❋ ❋

Looking back, I now see that everything I learned from Thomas Berry over the next ten years was grounded in that experience on the Creeping Cedar Trail in which I became aware of a penetration into a deeper dimension of reality …

In the weeks that followed my walk with Thomas, I spent time in the woods remembering my past relationship to the land that I had lived on for thirty-two years, while at the same time seeking to develop a new intimacy with it. During those years now past, my relationship with the land had been largely one of appreciation as a backdrop for family activities.

Memories arose of major projects that my husband and sons had undertaken: the building of fences, roads, trails, and the creation of a pond came to mind, along with stories of creatures we had befriended or who had befriended us, like the baby raccoons we found swimming in the pond one evening. We pulled them up onto our paddleboat and they ended up living with us for months. And the little black calf, born unexpectedly in the middle of January, who was rejected by its mother and left for our family to care for.

I recalled family rituals: the rope swing that hung high over the creek that had to be reinstated each spring, Fourth of July celebrations with fireworks over the pond in front of the farmhouse, Christmas carols around the tree in the Great Room, and nights of star gazing from the deck …

And then with grief I remembered seeing my husband, a deeply private soul, leaving his bedroom confinement one day near the end of his life to slip outside with his feeding tube in the pocket of his bathrobe, so that he could touch the bark of the trees and listen to the sounds of the birds which he recorded on a small tape recorder. It was as if he was memorizing—learning by heart—this place that he had so dearly loved before his soaring spirit began its final journey.

And now, in this new phase of my life, Thomas Berry was offering a way to "see" this land, this earth, with new eyes, in a "mutually enhancing" relationship that would be life-changing and life-giving.

I set out on daily walks and began to "see" more of the particularity of trees I had known for so long, the pattern of their bark, the "feel" of their muscled trunks, the shape of their leaves, and their relationships to other trees near by. I began to be aware of an inner connection to them as old friends. I began to perceive qualities of the earth that I had never been aware of before: the courage of the tiny wood violet bravely positioned in the middle of a trail where anyone could snuff out its life with a misplaced footstep, the deep patience of the old familiar oak, the exuberance

*of fall mushrooms popping up in different colors. I was begin-
ning to sense a new reciprocity between myself and the natural world
by not seeing it simply as a backdrop for human activity. Instead I
was seeing the integrity and dignity of each unique part of it. Everything, and everyone, I was beginning to realize, was in the process
of transformation as every death gives way to new life.*

*I looked forward to speaking further with Thomas about these
things.*

Chapter Two

A Sense of the Sacred

My next conversation with Thomas Berry took place again at the Green Valley Grill in November of 1999, not long after our walk at Timberlake. I remember it as a cold but cloudless day; the sun was shining through the restaurant's long windows as I made my way to his booth, and I was aware of the soft notes of classical music in the background. Thomas was again cheerfully munching on the hard rolls that he loved and he rose to greet me with his usual depth of kindness that was not tacked on for the moment but a substance fully integrated.

We sat down and the waitperson took our drink order and then asked if we were ready to order our dinners. Thomas carefully explained that we would place our menus on the edge of the table when we were ready. Turning back to me, Thomas opened up the conversation with "How's yourself?"

This allowed me to tell him about my changing perceptions of the natural world and to ask him questions about the moment of epiphany that I had witnessed in the woods at Timberlake a month earlier. I had a small notebook and a pen that I wore on a chain around my neck and I was all ready to take notes, which Thomas liked to see.

As I shared some of my recent experiences in the woods, Thomas listened with his usual complete attention and then answered very slowly and deliberately: "You are beginning to remember what has been forgotten: the inner life of humans and the outer life of the natural world. The two go together. The natural world activates the spirit in our minds. We have a natural bond of intimacy with the natural world; something within us goes out to meet every living thing."

I asked him if he was referring to the "mutually enhancing relationship" he had spoken of at our dinner in August and he nodded, answering that our acknowledgment of the distinctive qualities of the earth strengthens our spirits.

As he spoke, I wrote, "We receive from the natural world, we acknowledge it, and as we do so, we receive again. The 'natural bond of intimacy' is forged."

When I read this back to Thomas, he added, "And we establish a *relationship* with the natural world instead of an identity *over* and *against* it which separates the part from the whole." Then he spoke so softly I had to lean forward to hear him: "We recover intimate modes of Divine presence. We recover our souls."

My mind went to the wood violet that I had encountered on the trail and I felt the depth of his understanding, for there was a moment in which I had felt the very essence of that tiny flower, a tender love for it and an inner response from it as I knelt down beside it on the path. I remembered a feeling of being "held" in that moment and expressed this to Thomas.

"We discover our fulfillment in those deeper moments in which we feel our oneness with the universe," he said. "In those moments we feel the intimacy, the unity of our relationship to all things and to the Divine."

I asked Thomas if that had been his experience on the day I handed him the sprig of creeping cedar on the trail at Timberlake. He nodded. "The sense of the sacred is at the heart of it all," he said, repeating with emphasis what he had said to me on our walk. "The sacred is that which evokes wonder, the natural world is that mysterious presence that we refer to as the Divine. We find it as we celebrate the wonder of existence in the dawn, the midday, the closing of the day, in acknowledging the water, wind, earth, trees. We find it as we stop and experience the full depth of the natural world as we look at it, listen to it, feel it in numinous moments in which, through our intuitive awareness, we come into its mystery. We enter into hidden realms of the natural world and they enter into us.

"Understanding and appreciation are activated within us which take us to the world of the sacred. That is what we have forgotten; that is what you are remembering. Only a sense of the sacred can save us. It has been said that, "we will only save what we love." I add, "and we will only love that which we regard as sacred."

I asked him, "What is it within the human soul that allows this sense of the sacred to arise?"

Thomas paused for quite a long while before choosing the most appropriate response. "In Confucianism there is a concept known as *Jen* (pronounced Ren), which is a way of speaking of qualities latent in the depths of oneself; it is a special way of feeling, of sympathetic communion. A compassion arises from the basic tendencies of our hearts as we journey to the center of our being where Love resides. We discover that we have within us a heavenly-endowed nature in this process, 'shoots of goodness,' I call them, that need cultivation. We have a basic drive toward goodness and Life itself that needs to be acknowledged."

"Does everyone have this 'sense of the sacred?'" I asked him.

"Everyone has the capacity for it," he replied, "but it must be cultivated. The first thing is to become aware outside oneself. We need instructions in the otherness of existence. The human and the natural world come together in a special way in which the universe is present in a moment of epiphany.

"The sense of the sacred affixes within us in response to the natural world. It is all there in a unity that is different for everyone. The Divine is present in every moment." And then he added quietly, "In the sacred, all opposites are reconciled."

Then changing the mood, Thomas said with a grin, "Next time we get together, I'll tell you an immense story of the sacred."

After looking over our menus, Thomas put them on the corner of the table to signal the waitperson that we were ready to order. For dessert he ordered with great delight one crème brûlée with two spoons, a ritual that was to be repeated with every meal shared at the Green Valley Grill.

Afterward he walked me to my car and waited on the curb until I pulled out of the parking lot waving goodbye as I watched in my rear view mirror. When I arrived home, there was a message on my answering machine: "Carolyn, this is Thomas. Call and tell me you're home safe."

❋ ❋ ❋ ❋ ❋ ❋

Following this meeting with Thomas Berry, I began a practice of taking notes from our conversations into the woods with me, along with my journal in an attempt to connect more deeply to an understanding of the human-earth relationship. I felt the truth of what he was saying about a sense of the sacred as if I had always known it somehow, but not at a conscious level; I was aware that it had existed as a deep feeling that had been present at crucial moments in my life but had never been aware of the capacity to "cultivate" it.

Thomas had said, "What has been forgotten is the inner life of humans and the outer life of the natural world. The two go together." That was revelatory to me for he was saying that inner and outer landscapes were connected, that we have "a natural bond of intimacy with the natural world," and that "something within us goes out to meet every living thing."

I thought again of the little wood violet and its vulnerability in the middle of a trail where it could be easily trampled. My compassionate response to the tiny flower made me remember Thomas also saying, "We have within us a special way of feeling, of sympathetic communion, 'shoots of goodness,' that need to be cultivated."

Thomas had said, "The first thing is to become aware outside yourself." But this was not so easy to do. The conditioned mind has its own agenda, its habits, its categories, its arguments for what one should and shouldn't do with one's time. Then there are the very real responsibilities that inexorably press upon one's life. Taking time out to "cultivate" the sacred seemed like an unusual task, and yet intuitively I knew it was one I must undertake, that everything I was to learn at this time must come out of my own experience in conjunction with the wisdom that Thomas Berry was sharing with me.

I walked silently in the woods, realizing how self-absorbed were all my thoughts. Then I stopped and tried to take in the "otherness" of the tree before me. It was an old pine tree with bent limbs from its cramped position on a hill between two others, yet still bending upward toward the light. As I became more still, I began to notice the movement of water on the pond below with ripples of an unknown origin. I noticed the movement of leaves in the trees above the pond. Then I became aware of movement all around me as a slight breeze came along and everything seemed to join in a cosmic dance.

Sound became the next theme with tiny insect sounds close by and large bird sounds farther away. I turned my gaze to look slowly around me and realized that I was seeing anew this place that I had lived in and loved for so long.

I wrote in my journal: "There is another sacred world in this world that I will come to know. Perhaps we see what we are looking for. Perhaps what we need is a new way of seeing."

Chapter Three

The Universe Story

The Green Valley Grill was unusually quiet at my next dinner meeting with Thomas. It was winter now with the earth silent and an appropriate time to hear the story he had promised to tell me.

When I arrived, Thomas was already there as before, wearing his blue jacket and in his favorite booth munching on hard rolls. I hurried to reach him before he had to get up to greet me, and once again felt the largess of his welcome as he took both my hands and we both chuckled a bit in delight at coming together again. In all the years I spent time with Thomas I never forgot the privilege of being with him. I was beginning to see that through his companionship and the thoughts he was sharing with me, I was beginning to find a new purposefulness and energy for rebuilding my life. I longed to further understand Thomas' thinking so I could share it with others.

The waitperson came and Thomas ordered wine for us, then moved the dinner menus to the wall indicating that there was to be a long conversation before ordering food. I was prepared with my pen and notebook.

He began with his customary: "How's yourself and what's going on out your way?"

I gave him a brief update on the work we were doing, founding an organization at Timberlake to bring children into a personal relationship with the natural world and he nodded his pleasure. Then I reminded Thomas that he had promised to tell me "an immense sacred story" that evening.

He began very slowly and deliberately: "It is a very ancient sacred story that must be remembered anew at this time. It is a story of our time and of the emergence of the universe. It is a story that from the beginning has been both spiritual as well as physical, subjective as well as objective. Science has given us quantitative evidence of the physical dimension. What has been left out is the psychic-spiritual dimension. We can now outline with precision the unfolding of the universe during its earliest moments of origin. But the literal story of the universe reduces it to physical measurement; what has been omitted is the greater story of the Mystery of the universe that cannot be reduced. The psychic-spiritual is emerging now. Our genetic coding verifies that we inherit both a physical and a psychic-spiritual dimension."

Thomas went on to say that this is a new sacred story of the immense cosmic-human-earth process, and emphasized that we now have empirical evidence from science that can confirm it and religious understandings that can consecrate it, yet it is larger than both. It is an epic story that brings a deep reverence and respect for all life processes that are both physical and spiritual. It is a story of hope that can give us an expanded context for our lives and new understanding and direction for both the individual and the future of the earth at this critical time in history.

I remember imagining in that moment, that instead of sitting within the ancient fire circle of a shaman with the howling cry of a wolf echoing in the night, I was about to hear Thomas' story in the cathedral-like Green Valley Grill with its high ceilings and with Brahms' majestic Fourth Symphony playing in the background. Somehow it seemed like an appropriate contemporary setting for what the Apache called "telling the holiness." I shared the image with Thomas and he smiled and shrugged his shoulders slightly to acknowledge it.

I can only try to relate the following in this written form, fully aware that it is inadequate to describe what came next, because the story Thomas Berry shared with me on that winter evening seemed to emerge from deep *within* the universe itself. Thomas invited me into the vast domain of cosmic time in which he was completely at home. With a voice filled with great reverence and deep love he began to describe the moment of the first primordial flaring forth of the universe and then the slow, slow, slow gradual unfolding of the Mystery which contained within itself "a deep latent purposefulness" as it unfurled for billions of years.

He related the wonder and magnificence of the huge cosmic drama that began with the shaping of the first generation of stars within galaxies to the collapse of those stars, which produced the supernova moment that brought into being the entire array of elements that made life possible on earth and from which the hidden purposefulness began to reveal itself. Through Thomas' further description of the transformational journey of the universe he illumined the miracle of the birth of a new star, which became our sun surrounded by planets. As the immense creative process continued, Earth came into existence.

Thomas paused for a moment in sheer wonderment as if hearing the sacred story anew for the first time in his own speaking of it. After a few moments he went on to marvel at the picture of the earth groping its way forward, finding its proper distance from the sun and moon, and surviving the transformations brought about by the volcanic explosions that led to the atmosphere, the seas, and the continents rising above the water. Then on to the emergence of life and "the wonder of existence in the living cell." With increasing intensity and awe, Thomas told of the miracle of the living cell that contains the power of human consciousness and memory, and thus, the capacity through time for the organism to both learn from its achievements and correct its mistakes.

He described crucial moments in earth's evolution, including one in particular in which if the rate of expansion had been slower, the universe would have collapsed; if it had expanded more quickly, the universe would have exploded. But, Thomas emphasized, *the life generating purposefulness* behind the sacred story allowed the expansion to continue at exactly the right rate to create the conditions for the human soul to be born.

"Science discusses the universe in terms of matter," he interjected into his narrative, "but it doesn't discuss causes of the universe in terms of *purpose*. The universe must be seen beyond itself in terms of the *purpose* of a creative principle; science can give us nothing beyond the physical universe."

Thomas went on to describe the Paleozoic and Mesozoic eras, but particularly the "lyric" Cenozoic era when flowers, trees, birds and mammals "came into their greatest splendor." Through its miraculous sequence of transformations, the universe was revealing a very particular emergent pattern directed toward human life on earth. The universe, Thomas said, was beginning to reveal its purposefulness in a life principle that carried within itself "a tendency toward greater and greater differentiation, a deepening spontaneity, and an evermore intimate self-bonding of its components."

In Thomas' "telling of the holiness," one process could be seen at work through the immense diversity of all creation that included creatures, plants and humans as members of a vast interconnected earth community. As he spoke, I could see that this was the new sacred story of the universe.

"Now," Thomas went on, "we know conclusively from science that the universe is an irreversible emergent process and *is continuing to expand;* that it is moving from lesser to greater complexity and from lesser to greater consciousness." He then added, "*We are part of it all and integral with it.* The human story and the universe story is a single sacred story with the Divine as its origin and destiny. We can discern the numinous guidance that has accompanied the universe and the individual through all its catastrophes and all its transformations."

Then Thomas spoke these words very softly: "And through it all, a Powerful Loving Voice spoke through every cosmic activity."

Thomas paused here for me to try to take in the magnitude of what he was saying and the implications for our personal lives. I told him what I was thinking and he responded by saying, "Each of us bears within us these transformations of the universe. This is the personal sacred story of each individual within the great sacred story of the universe; they cannot be separated. Each of us goes through our own stages of transformation in which new levels of being emerge through the urgency of self-transcendence, and each of us is under the same numinous guidance. You have only to look back at earlier realities in your own evolving story to remember the spiritual forces that have worked in your behalf to overcome every obstacle."

As Thomas spoke I was able to recall the many moments of mysterious spiritual help that had come for me in times of great difficulty and how I had felt moved to new levels of consciousness through each lesson learned. I shared this with Thomas and he commented, "We are organized to grow on."

He then repeated what he had said in the beginning, "The universe is both spiritual as well as physical, which must be remembered at this time. Science can give us much, but it cannot give us a sense of purpose and meaning or a sense of the sacred. The universe is a manifestation of the mystery of the Divine and everything and everyone in the universe is an aspect of the Divine."

Thomas went on to expand the story of human development through a Primal Phase and a Civilizational Phase, tracing within each a sense of the sacred, which was present when the human and the cosmic were in "intimate rapport." Numinous moments of dawn and dusk were celebrated through rituals and ceremonies, and humans saw themselves as integral with the earth, living in ever-renewing seasons of life in a spatial context that provided an understanding of one's place within the whole universe, and a commitment to the cosmological order in which everything is a part.

He then recounted the beginnings of the loss of the sacred when a deeper commitment was given to a *linear historical* order. The experience of the Divine in the present moment was lost along with our personal relationship to the natural world. He then swept through history from the mid-fourteenth century when the horrors of the Black Death prompted a desire for transcendence away from the natural world, and a sense of presence was lost as man made efforts to control the environment. In subsequent centuries, the earth was seen as a resource for the development of the mechanistic, the industrial and the technological. "Intimacy with the natural world," he said, "gave way to using the earth for political and economic domination."

Thomas spoke with great grief in his voice of the "shuddering effects" of the transformations continuing to take place in the present time with the tragic consequences for all of life, human and non-humans. "What is happening in our times," he said, "is not just another historical transition or cultural change. The devastation of the planet that we are bringing about is negating some millions, even billions of years of past development on earth. We are within a momentous period of change unparalleled in the four and a half billions years of earth history. We have changed the chemistry of the planet, the bio-systems of the planet, the geology of the planet, and now even the ozone layer. We are now in the terminal phase of the Cenozoic era. We are destroying the very basis on which we depend."

We both fell silent after that for what seemed like a very long period.

Finally, Thomas began to speak very softly and slowly so that I could take down every word: "We are living in a time of historic confusion in which the sacred story has been forgotten and must be remembered anew; the survival of both the natural world and the human depend upon it. Our fate and the fate of the planet is identical. We must shift from an entirely human centered view of our existence to a realization that the earth is a communion of subjects, a oneness of which we are all a part. It is *not* a collection of objects for our use. We must enter into a new human-earth-Divine relationship within a new sacred story that is emerging to meet the barrenness of this time."

I saw that Thomas was ready to stop, but he thought of something he wanted to add: "We are here to remedy time before it is too late, and the sacred story of the evolution of the universe teaches us that we are capable of serving life's purpose *if we can only learn to see it.*"

He then suggested we look at the menus and order our food. After dinner Thomas again ordered the crème brûlée with two spoons and concluded by saying, "We'll talk more about this next time after you've had a chance to reflect. You have to make all of these things your own in your own way and then you can share them with others. That's how we evolve."

He walked me to my car as before and was still standing there waving goodbye when I looked back. When I returned home, there was his usual message on my answering machine: "Carolyn, this is Thomas. Call and let me know you're home safe."

Somehow I was beginning to feel that I was.

※ ※ ※ ※ ※ ※

In the days and weeks that followed, I tried to take in the magnitude of Thomas' universe story. Each day I explored ways to discover my own understanding of it and to somehow become a vessel to contain and nurture its development as Thomas had advised. I read and re-read my notes so as not to forget any part.

From the heart of the universe, as it seemed to me in retrospect, the sacred story took me from the primordial flaring forth of the Mystery of the universe to a vision of galaxies forming, earth, air, land and water interacting in the energy of the sun, the moon taking its place, continents arising, and all within an overall patterning that revealed a Divine Power and a purposefulness that ended in humankind as its most complete expression.

It was not only the immensity of the universe story that I was trying to absorb, but also Thomas as the storyteller. In my imagination they were one. Thomas seemed to be living within the story in a deep personal equilibrium with it, as if he were continually aligned with the very heartbeat of the universe—as if the universe was speaking through him. His scholarship was part of it, but the story seemed to come first from a contemplative mind supported by an analytical mind. It also included a numinous dimension, a "Divine Love" that set all things in motion from the beginning and continued to move the sun, moon and stars in Divine order. Thomas Berry was the consummate storyteller behind the story who was able to convey the deepest intentions of the universe through every word, gesture and tone, somehow linking the temporal with the eternal.

I could see how the new sacred story could bring science and religion, so long separated, into a new and comprehensive synthesis, with each embracing the other in a cosmology larger than either. Science, having left out the sacred, and religion, having left out science, were coming together through the new story to begin healing all that had been ravaging the earth in our time.

As Thomas explained it, by understanding the gravitational bondedness of all components to each other, as science understands it, or as the communion of all living things with one another as viewed in spiritual terms, the human community could let go of the sense of separation from the whole that has so plagued the structure of modern thought with its devastating consequences.

Taking this story in deeply could begin to change our practices of relating to one another, human and non-human, as we make real our eternal connections to one another and accept that every single life force is an expression of One Creator and that we are all related through that same Source.

I made a note to ask Thomas to speak more about relationships in the context of the new sacred story.

I could dimly begin to see the staggering implications for a new understanding of the universe and the individual in a time that was demanding it; the universe through a sequence of transformations always moving the life principle forward, and we as part of the universe, "organized," as Thomas put it, to participate in that emerging process. But how to participate seemed to be the question, and Thomas, it seemed, was offering a new direction, a direction of inner evolution, spiritual evolution, as we "grope" our way forward to meet the exigencies of our times.

Thomas' statements that "the universe is spiritual as well as physical" and that "we inherit both dimensions through our genetic coding" could give us strength to claim the validity of our own innate spirituality, so long denied. This acknowledgment of both dimensions of human nature, the spiritual and the physical, could allow us to speak of the innerness of our lives and to share it more openly with others. It could allow us to speak of Love at the very core of our being as it evolves or "unfurls," as the dictionary defines "evolve." It could even allow us to be bold and speak of the evolution of Love as each of us has come to know it, allowing us to share our individual stories of faith within the great sacred story of faith that could help us grow and heal in this time of "historic confusion."

I took many walks in the woods "carrying" the new sacred story in my mind and heart. I began to see with deepening gratitude the inter-communion of trees and plants and creatures that the Creator as origin and destiny of the long creative process of evolution had brought forth for billions of years, and I wondered how we on this earth could carelessly participate in the present "extinction spasm of our times." Surely it was time for us to awaken in all our complexity and unity to see that we are one single earth community that lives or dies together. I remembered that the "sprouts of goodness" are within us all if we can cultivate them and vowed to nurture the delicate seeds of new understanding that I was being given.

I became keenly aware of the emerging process of all about me in the natural world as I saw an old tree trunk dissolving right next to a new patch of moss that was arising. I saw this, too, in all the various stages of my life as old patterns dissolved to make room for new ones in the continual movement of transformation. This dissolving and coming back together again, this forming is the basis of all life, all fertility. I must trust this ever-renewing process of self-renewal in my own life, I thought, and I saw that it could even replace fear of the future.

I was beginning to learn from the earth.

In the story of the universe, the primordial emergence was the beginning of the earth's story. It was also the beginning of the personal story for each of us, since the story of the universe is the story of each individual within it. That story is constantly "unfurling" in our lives if we can just see it. We are here to transform the past with the miracle of the human cell and its capacity to learn from its mistakes along with the numinous guidance that has also accompanied the immense journey. It requires our capacity for reflection and a commitment to the universe ... not a small undertaking, but in view of this critical juncture in human history, it is the only way forward.

Oliver Wendell Holmes said, "The mind once stretched to a new idea never goes back to its original dimensions." Thomas Berry was stretching our minds and enlarging our hearts with the new sacred story so that we could never go backward but only forward in learning to see the whole earth as one sacred community that lives or dies together. Everything we do and say and think affects the whole.

The old story of separateness has been disproved by science. There is a gravitational bond that connects us all. Becoming aware of that "bond of intimacy" in the new sacred story can bring us into communion with all living things.

Much to ponder ...

Chapter Four

Relationships

Our next conversation was in early spring, a March moment in North Carolina where crocus and daffodils announce new beginnings. The sun over the pond was reflected by sparkles on the water and the air was clear and pure and unseasonably warm on this particular afternoon. As I waited for Thomas to arrive at the TreeHouse, the dwelling place on the land for our children's programs, I was grateful to be able to sit outside on the deck overlooking the woods for our conversation that day.

I had called Thomas and requested a time to meet to ask him further questions about relationships in the context of the new sacred story. He replied, "I love questions. Questions are the way civilizations move forward!" He didn't add that he only loved *big* questions such as "What is the meaning of existence?" or "What is the purpose of time?" As Thomas' niece Ann Berry Somers once said, "Uncle Brother," as the family called him, "never tarried in small talk."

I was beginning to see, as I daily pondered the new sacred story of the universe, that an enlarged awareness was dawning in my soul. I was living more deeply into what Abraham Joshua Heschel called "radical amazement" of the natural world as I considered its cosmic history on my daily walks.

I was realizing that each time I met with Thomas another layer of understanding was possible and I longed to learn more.

He arrived about mid-afternoon and parked his car outside the TreeHouse, and dropped out of it without looking back, doubtlessly leaving his keys. (One time I asked him if he was ever concerned about the theft of his car and he replied, "No, if someone else needs it, they can have it!" Apparently, no one ever did.)

I remember feeling much joy in anticipation of our conversation and imagined that the flowers, trees and creatures on the land were also welcoming his presence that day. Thomas loped up the steps to the TreeHouse and expressed pleasure in being at Timberlake again as we proceeded to the deck to settle in with glasses of iced tea.

Thomas opened up the conversation with "So you've had a chance to reflect on all we talked about?"

"Yes," I responded, "and I need to understand more about relationships as I try to integrate the new story that includes both physical and psychic-spiritual dimensions."

I waited for his response, which came after a very long silence as he slowly gathered his thoughts in a way that would be most helpful. I was ready to take copious notes.

"The epic of evolution," Thomas finally began, "calls for a new sense of relationships. We are now in a numinous integrative phase as we seek to understand ourselves in the context of an emerging cosmic-human-earth process. In the new sacred story, relationships are the primary context of existence. We are in the third age of relationships in our human evolution. The first was the human-Divine relationship, the second was the human-human relationship, and now the third must be the human-earth-Divine relationship as we discover our bond of intimacy with all living forms and recognize the companionship of the abiding numinous presence.

"We have had little attraction toward a shared communion existence within the greater world of living forms. We hardly think of ourselves within a multi-species community. But we are ready to receive the cosmos now because of the desperation of our situation, the loss of animals and plants and aspects of the universe." He said this with grief in his voice.

He paused for another very long moment and then went on: "We begin with an awareness that science has given us of the gravitational bonding within the universe itself and within each of its components, and the intimate presence of each component of the universe with other components, a mystical attraction, you might say. The deeper meaning of this is not generally understood as we continue to see the radical discontinuity between humans and non-humans, which has led to humans' savage assault on the earth. The earth has been seen as a collection of objects to be *used* instead of as a communion of subjects of which we are all a part."

I had to stop and ask Thomas to further explain this phrase that he used so often.

"An object," he said, "is something that is separate from oneself and can be acted upon, whereas a subject is a primary referent. An object is an 'it,' different from ourselves, which we feel we can manipulate or destroy, while a subject is that with which we identify, but are not identical to, that we respect and revere."

He went on to explain that as we shift to identifying ourselves with one another as part of a total earth community that includes all living forms, our actions change in alignment with our new understanding. Thomas then shared with me a vision of the whole sacred universe as one single coherent community with all elements in total interdependence with one another; every human, creature, tree, plant and star unique, and each with its place within the whole with a particular function to perform that all the others depended upon. Within his vision I saw one earth community in which all elements were whole and yet all were contained within the larger whole of the universe. It was indeed a "communion"—a union—of subjects, not a collection of separate random objects.

I sat for a long moment trying to take this all in, and then finally replied that if we could learn to hold this vision for ourselves, the deep separation between the human and the non-human could be healed. It was an overwhelming thought to me on that March afternoon on the deck of the TreeHouse to imagine the considerable restructuring of the psyche that would need to happen to fully absorb that vision and live out of it.

I told Thomas what I was thinking and he replied, "That transformation is already happening now. We are in a convulsive moment of history in which it is beginning to be understood that the role and rationale and mission of the human is in communion with all living forms." He waved his arm toward the woods. "We are actually in a mystical rapport with these budding trees, the song birds, the graciousness of this sun, the amazing diversity of it all, but we need to acknowledge the sacredness of our relationship, our *communion* with the earth, the universe and the Divine." With these words, I remembered the holiness of the moment I had experienced with Thomas on the Creeping Cedar Trail months earlier.

We sat silently for a while before Thomas continued telling me that he was intent upon expressing the knowledge of our bondedness in subjective and qualitative ways that are omitted in the language of science. I was beginning to see that Thomas was integrating the spiritual dimension of the universe into everything he was teaching. When I mentioned this, he simply nodded and said that we need both kinds of knowing now that we understand the universe to be both physical and psychic-spiritual.

"The scientific story," he said, "must be accompanied by a spiritual story, for we have become strangers to the natural world except in a scientific way. Through literal thinking we lose a sense of the sacred, but we also lose a sense of the universe. Words of love, beauty, wonder, and goodness are not scientific words. Scientific words are ways of analyzing and lead to *using* the earth as a resource, which has become our ultimate judgment. That's why I say that science needs to function *within* a cosmology, not as if it *is* a cosmology."

Thomas paused to sip his iced tea and to give us both time to take this in before continuing: "I like to use the terms 'subjectivity, differentiation, and communion' to express these thoughts, which are actually laws of the universe that hold all things together. I've told you before that in ancient China this was known as *jen*, pronounced 'ren,' *the interior binding force of the universe,* a vision that was the guiding force behind their cultivation of 'a sympathetic presence' of all things to each other. It described an order of goodness, love and compassion mutually beneficial for all."

I urged Thomas to help me better understand these three terms.

"*Subjectivity* helps us understand that every being has its own interior, its own mystery, its numinous aspect, 'the authenticity at the heart of every being,' as it is said in Confucianism. It is this interiority that attunes us to the deeper mystery of things and opens us to the sacred presence within each reality of the universe. This is an understanding that was lost in the process of 'progress,' and the vast mythic, symbolic world with all its pervasive numinous qualities was also nearly lost entirely.

"Now in these evolutionary times there is an ever-increasing awakening of interior consciousness. A reversal has begun as the interior, subjective, spiritual dimension of the entire cosmic order is being integrated as the basic foundation of the new sacred story."

Thomas then defined *differentiation* with great care by returning to his vision of a whole coherent universe directed toward expressing a vast multiplicity of forms of "immense variety within unity as the original primordial energy dispersed itself."

In a lyrical and poetic fashion he described the most min-
utest atomic structures of plants, animals and human forms to
show the remarkable aim of the universe in creating astonishing
differences in both quantitative and qualitative ways. "Human
individuals differ from each other more extensively than in any
other realm of known reality, but each form has its own identity, its dignity, its inner spontaneity, its sacred dimension. The
natural world has its own meaning within itself; it is not the
meaning humans give to it. Consciousness comes when we
awaken to an understanding of the richness of the diversity of it
all."

"And what about communion?" I asked him.

"The third term, *communion,* is meant to understand the
interrelationship of the universe within itself and the inter-
connectedness of each part with the whole—the 'interior binding
force of the universe.' It is meant to express what is the deepest
reality in all the universe, that capacity for mutual indwelling
of each reality with every other reality.

"First, we must be in communion with our own deeper interior subjective selves, then with the larger community of life,
and then with the universal order of things. Bonding then refers
not just to the physical, but to the natural spiritual bond of intimacy we feel with all living forms that is mystical and cov-
enantal.

"We are intimately bonded with everything all the way out
to the stars," he said with a smile. "Quantum physics tell us that
every atom influences every other atom without a known signal
passing through the intervening space. I like to say we are not

ourselves without everything and everyone else," he concluded, speaking a phrase I was to hear him repeat many times throughout the years.

There was a momentary pause for which I was grateful, as I needed to breathe out from the intensity of all that Thomas was offering. He noted this with his usual deep kindness and said with a grin, "This is a subject for a lifetime. Let's go for a walk."

It was approaching sunset as we walked slowly and silently to the edge of a large field surrounded by tall pines. The sun in the west was wreathing the land in deepening shades of orange and pink. Thomas spoke softly, "We are being held in the compassionate arc of the universe."

When we returned to the TreeHouse, I served our supper of vegetable soup and bread at the long kitchen table and then reopened the conversation: "Thomas, I need help understanding how to practice seeing relationships in the ways you described."

He nodded and replied, "Anything one comes to know has to be understood and it has to be practiced for a person to come to a new world of meaning. I like what Tielhard said about seeing: 'Seeing. One could say that the whole of life lies in seeing.' He also said, 'The history of the living world can be reduced to the elaboration of ever more perfect eyes at the heart of a cosmos where it is always possible to discern more. See or perish. This is the situation imposed on every element of the universe by the gift of existence.'"

He paused to let me take this in before continuing. "For subjectivity, one must first acquire a capacity for interior presence to oneself. Through contemplation one sinks deeply into the subjectivity of one's own being to deepen one's personal sacred center. This becomes the deepening of the capacity for communion with all things. Through this practice we acknowledge our relationship to the whole of which we are a part; we acknowledge that we are integral with the universe. We then begin to see, to awaken to the universe in all its magnificent differentiation and a new consciousness comes with an understanding of the depth and diversity of things. We become truly present to other modes of being."

Then he repeated these words from our earlier conversations, words that I knew I would need to absorb over and over to integrate their meaning: "As we practice this way of seeing, we come into a mutually enhancing relationship with everything and everyone that strengthens the individual through the distinctive quality of things that brings about communion. This creates a deep bond of intimacy that is invisible but knowable, a presence that is palpable."

I could tell that Thomas was about to conclude when he said: "Subjectivity and differentiation are fulfilled in communion. By enlarging our hearts and minds to include every living thing, we participate in the functioning of the universe and the Divine order of things with deeper and deeper intimacy. It is our destiny now in the twenty-first century to develop this capacity for communion on new and more comprehensive levels. We are being changed. We are being transformed to see everything in its true proportion. We are being driven down to the heart with its radical interior tendencies."

"Thomas," I said, "aren't you really speaking of love?"

"Love," he said simply, "is an inner presence to all things."

The evening ended and I walked Thomas to his car. This time I stood waving goodbye as he drove out of sight.

❋ ❋ ❋ ❋ ❋ ❋

So much to take in ... I felt the great gift of his transmission through these conversations on the one hand and my own inade-quacies in receiving it on the other. Still I knew in my soul that Thomas Berry's understanding would bring new meaning into this present time and that I must one day share it with others.

From my notes I began summarizing our time together. I had asked Thomas to speak about relationships following his evening of telling me the new sacred story of the universe, and he commented that in the epic of evolution there was emerging a new sense of relationships as "the primary context of existence."

He validated my question and then placed it within the huge evolutionary context by saying that we are now in the third age of relationships, that of the human-earth-Divine relationship in which we are called to be in communion with all living forms, and to recognize the companionship of the "numinous, abiding presence" as we do. He then went on to say that science gives us an understanding of the relationship with all things through the gravitational bonding of all particles, but that a deeper spiritual meaning of a communion of subjects must be integrated if we are to halt the "savage assault on the earth."

Thomas shared his vision of the universe in which all elements were seen in their amazing diversity in interdependency

*throughout as a way of explaining his use of the word "commun-
ion," "with oneness" as the word is defined. I could see that Thomas
was integrating a spiritual dimension into the story through language
that science could not speak. By so doing, he was moving us out of
our entrapment for the past centuries in which the language of the
mechanical, the industrial, and the technological had kept us in
bondage. As he brought matter and spirit together, a leap in consciousness was taking place. New understanding was being born.*

*In the weeks that followed our meeting at the TreeHouse, I
started practicing the inward and outward journeys of subjectivity,
differentiation and communion to develop an understanding out
of my own experiences. I practiced a morning meditation that
began with an awareness of the rising sun followed by the rising
of mists over the pond, and then sought to move downward into
the "radical tendencies of the heart" to remember the Divine purposefulness that brought forth all of life and to find inner stillness
there.*

*The effort was toward a holding of the love that was there as
an inner presence, and of being held by it in return. As time went
on, I practiced remembering ... mountains, plains, rivers, forests,
creatures, as well as all dearly loved family members and friends
... including the great sea of humanity suffering from their separation from the earth, the universe, the Divine, the soul.*

*I continued my trail walks and began to really see the vast and
infinite variety in patterns, colors, textures, the diversity of plants and
creatures, and the one life force that we all shared in common.
Thomas' words that "subjectivity and differentiation are fulfilled
in communion" began to reveal themselves to me. I began to under-*

stand how we could see everything in "its true proportion" by coming into a bond of intimacy with the universe. "Love as an inner presence to all things" was the "interior binding force of the universe" that holds all things together. It was still speaking to us as it had since the beginning of the mysterious long and slow evolutionary process with Life as its goal.

I looked up the word "radical" in the dictionary and discovered it had two meanings: one, "Arising from or going to a root or a source; fundamental, basic," and two, "Carried to the farthest limit; extreme, sweeping." Thomas was saying that "we are being driven down to the heart with its radical interior tendencies" which I interpreted to mean that the direction of the heart is toward the root, or the source of all things, which is the Divine.

I could see we were being transformed; we were being driven down now in this "convulsive" period of the twenty-first century by our circumstances as human beings on earth at this time, to the interior life of the heart, which was taking us, through its natural drift, toward the Source of our very being, which is God.

The image that came to mind was of being moved along in the deep current of life as in a canoe or kayak in swiftly moving water. There was no need to fear as long as we remembered the purposefulness and life force behind the movement, and the meaning that Thomas offered, "To see everything in its proper proportion."

I realized that instead of receiving certain answers to my questions, Thomas was offering me a larger context within which to consider them and the conceptual tools for finding them on my own. He was teaching, not what to see, but that I could learn to see. He was guiding me to discover my own truths about relation-

ships that were integral with the cosmic-human-earth process, and pointing me to the enlargement of heart, mind and soul, so required for our time.

As I continued to reflect on Thomas' thoughts, I remembered the Navajo shaman who placed a diseased patient on the ground and created a sand painting around him to give him a new context of order, a new larger story for his life within which his healing could take place.

This is what Thomas was providing and I was grateful.

Chapter Five

Relationships Continued

It was later in the spring when I received a call from Thomas asking if I could give him a ride the next morning to speak about the human-earth relationship at a pre-breakfast meeting of students and faculty at Guilford College. I was happy to do so and when we arrived at the college he insisted that I accompany him into the gathering.

Rather than giving a formal presentation, Thomas turned the moment into a simple conversation with those assembled in the college's dining hall. I noted that his complete ease with his subject and his very presence with the group brought a particular depth and intimacy into the room on that early morning in May. When students asked him questions, he replied with the quality of attention that I had experienced myself with a deep respect for both the questions and the questioners.

When it was over, we were invited to stay for breakfast, but Thomas declined. As we made our way back to the college parking lot, I assumed I would be taking him right home. Instead, Thomas said, "Let's go for a bagel!"

At his suggestion, I headed towards Bruegger's Bagel Shop. As we drove along I jokingly commented about his boldness in telling the new story of the universe to college students at eight o'clock in the morning. He responded by quoting Albert Einstein who said that the problems of our time could not be resolved at the same level at which they were created. The universe, Thomas said, was calling us to evolve to new levels of understanding.

"We need a new central focus to review the human situation," he continued as we got out of the car. "With the new sacred story of the universe, students can see the continuity of their own personal development in the prior development of the universe, the earth and all human history. This can activate a feeling of identity with the entire human venture." I fumbled for my notebook to remember this as I followed him into the bagel shop.

It turned out that in addition to the Green Valley Grill, Bruegger's Bagels on Battleground Avenue in Greensboro was another of Thomas Berry's favorite haunts. The manager greeted him with great joy as we approached, and served up his usual order of regular coffee and bagel with cream cheese without even being asked. Thomas made his way to his special table and I joined him.

As we settled in Thomas said, "Well, what question do you have for me today?"

I was surprised but not completely unprepared. I had been trying to deepen my meditative practice as he had suggested, paying closer attention on my daily walks to the immense differentiation of life in the woods. I was realizing that the practices of subjectivity, differentiation and communion were seeping into my human relationships and changing them as well. I had begun to appreciate temperamental differences in others instead of judging them, and had found a new sense of communion that I started to ask him about.

I scrambled for my notebook and pen as Thomas immediately replied, "From the earth we learn to understand the presence of all things to each other and this changes our human relationships. Learning to appreciate the universe is the key to all knowledge because it constitutes an *approach* to everything."

I knew he was going to expand on his perspectives and waited while he sipped his coffee and munched on his bagel. Finally, finding an inner place to start, Thomas began: "We are here to become integral with all our relations; I have said before that our role and rationale and mission is to be in communion with all living forms, both human and non-human. Remembering that from the beginning the universe has been spiritual as well as physical, it follows that everything and everyone has both a physical and spiritual dimension; there is an intrinsic goodness within all life. This is what we must keep in mind no matter what an individual is expressing at any given moment.

"There is a spark of divinity to be awakened within each one, a uniqueness that is an aspect of the sacred. All relationships carry that possibility. Someone or something must ignite that spark by loving the differences in each of us. In each meeting there is the mystery of the presence of another with whom one can discover new possibilities for life. Everyone and everything calls for recognition, the longing to be known for its special presence. To deprive any being of this sacred quality is to disrupt the total order of the universe.

"We depend upon others to give us ourselves by seeing our greater selves and bringing them forth through our relationships with them. We actually activate the sacred by recognizing it. There is a need for great interior development if this value is to be realized so that we can nurture one another's journey toward fulfillment. And people need to have a constant renewal of their bonding with one another."

Thomas paused then as he often did when he discovered new inner connections, as if to anchor them in his thoughts.

"The universe," he continued, "in its infinite creativity, places within each individual the longing for fulfillment, the longing of each living thing to find its unique sacred place which has the conditions for its particular fulfillment. Each individual is an expression of the universe with special intelligence, emotions and imagination. 'To be' is to be qualitatively different. Each individual has its own interior, its Self, its numinous aspect, which it searches for. Individuals seek identity in their own way to fulfill their uniqueness.

"This morning I was remembering that the students are searching for their uniqueness, their own authentic niche and that they need to be affirmed in their own trajectories. They are searching for a larger context for their lives and a sense of belonging to the universe, which they will never be able to find in a simulated world. They need new vision and hope that can come from a grounded idealism. They need to know that something new is happening, a new energy is coming into being and that everyone is needed with the unique gifts that each one of us brings. Young people today have a real historical role to play in the development of a new way of being. The disjunction with what is happening today is leading them to an awareness of the afflictions on earth and what they can do. They must ultimately discover the greater dimension of their own being within the community of the earth."

I asked Thomas about the sense of oneness I felt from the group of students listening to his talk, and he replied, "We are all a communion of subjects and when this is remembered it brings unity; a sense of mutual presence arises. The word 'presence' evokes a sense of immediacy, something taking place *now*. It is an intimate communion of thought; we become aware of a fluidity between ourselves and 'others' which is the sacred reality within us all. That is what you felt. There is a longing for this kind of communion and this intimate capacity for human relationships which human survival actually depends upon.

"Intimacy is what we are always adjusting in our relationships with one another as we learn to nurture one another's journeys. The whole evolutionary process depends upon communion. Without this fulfillment that each being finds in beings outside itself, nothing would ever happen in the entire world. There would be no elements, no molecules, no life, no consciousness. With communion, love is activated, universal presence to all things is established, a mutual indwelling occurs, which attracts all things and establishes order in the universe."

I started to say, "But there is so much disagreement—"

Thomas broke in to say, "Disagreement needs to be understood within the context of subjectivity, differentiation and communion in the universe. We can learn to see all difference within unity, that everything and everyone is bonded to everything and everyone else; there is a comprehensive coherence. If sharing is blocked, diversity is defeated. We can learn to see that opposing elements are necessary to contain us, and that our difficulties in relationships can be seen, not as demonic obstacles to be overcome, but as a discipline to evoke creativity. Difference is of real value in relationships; we even reflect in different modes of mind, imagination and emotions."

As I reflected on what he had just said, I realized that I needed more time to absorb his thinking and find ways to apply this in my daily living. I could also see that we were nearing the end of our time together, and as Thomas was finishing his coffee he was deciding on a way to conclude.

"To speak of relationships," he said, "is to acknowledge a mysterious bond, a connection that is invisible but knowable. Everything and everyone has an inner subjective identity and is bonded to everything and everyone else. Sameness is not meaningful; differences increase our capacity for communion, and qualitatively different relationships offer a mode of fulfillment that we need in a thousand different ways. Knowledge comes out of relationships. We need a celebration of differences that the universe teaches us!"

He smiled, pleased that the conversation was ending with a flourish! Then he stood up and added, "We have a natural bond of intimacy with all living forms which must be recovered at this 'convulsive' moment in history to which we are awakening."

I took him home to the dwelling he called his "Hermitage" and as I pulled away, I saw that he was standing at the foot of the stairs waving goodbye.

❋ ❋ ❋ ❋ ❋ ❋

In reviewing the notes from my bagel shop conversation with Thomas, I realized as usual that I had a great deal to absorb and integrate. The morning with him had revealed much: his delightful spontaneity with the students and faculty that awakened them to his message, his deep respect for each one there, and most of all his presence which seemed to unite the whole group. I could see the effect of his carrying the thought of the communion of subjects in the way the group responded to him. It was as if that belief evoked a spirit of willingness to feel themselves part of a whole.

Then I considered his words in the car about the universe calling us to evolve to new levels of understanding because the magnitude of our crisis could not be resolved at the same level at which it was created. I was beginning to understand that in our shift to seeing the earth as a communion of subjects, we would find all our relationships shifting, human and non-human.

If we really could accept that we are not ourselves without everything and everyone else, we could not continue to destroy one another and the earth. We would finally realize that we were one sacred community that lived or died together. I felt the overwhelming difficulty of accomplishing the inward shift that would be necessary until I remembered from the universe story that there is constant transformation always going on around and within us; we are always in the process of changing and becoming in an emergent universe. The challenge would be to continually align oneself in the direction of life's purposefulness.

Thomas' reminder that within each individual there is a spark of divinity that can be ignited through relationships puts us on notice of that possibility. And though I was aware that we all form limited images of each other according to our own moods and feelings that get fixed in the psyche from past encounters, I could see that Thomas was guiding us to see the sacred reality within all to help us move beyond our fixations. Accepting the spiritual dimension of the universe meant that we also had to accept the sacredness of all life—within ourselves and within one another. Realizing this fully could completely change the dynamics of all our human relationships; the very purpose of life would be to help each other come to the fulfillment of our unique place and cosmic assignment in the universe. If we could further remember that within every living thing there is a longing to find its own special place, its own fulfillment, we could live with greater understanding and compassion. That is what Thomas Berry was teaching in word and deed. He was inviting us into the inner contemplation of the whole of which we are a part and into inner and outer communion with one another, the whole earth, the universe and the Divine.

Thomas was meeting each situation from his enlargement of mind and heart. In his presence I could feel the small and petty dissolve within a context of greater truth, which allowed new energies to emerge. In every case he demonstrated how the develop-

ment of our understanding of the universe could bring this about, and lead us to new creativity by viewing the difficulties we experience at every turn through the light of the sacred story of the universe.

On my daily walks my prayer became, "Let the universe in all its marvelous differentiation teach me to celebrate differences in all the relationships in my life." For many weeks after my morning in the bagel shop with Thomas, I pondered the new understanding that had begun its transforming effects.

My practice of noticing was changing my perceptions and helping me keep in mind a "mutually enhancing relationship" when seeing a visiting crow, observing the first mushrooms of the season, watching the daily change of color as summer ended and fall began its bold display. Each was bringing me into a newer, deeper relationship with the land on which I lived. Each day giving and receiving were becoming one and were accompanied by a deep peace. I felt an inner connectedness each time I walked in the woods and I looked forward to talking with Thomas about this.

Chapter Six

Recovering the Soul

Another opportunity came in the summer of 2002 when I heard that Thomas had agreed to lead the Earth Elders Conference in Asheville, North Carolina. I called and asked if he needed another ride and he responded affirmatively with great delight.

I arrived at his Hermitage on the appointed day and noticed his slim black briefcase at the bottom of the steps that led up to his small apartment. I put it in the car and waited, fully expecting Thomas to come down the steps with another bag of some kind as the conference was to be several days long. When he appeared his hands were empty. I asked if he had more to bring down and he said, "Didn't you put my bag into your car already?"

I said, "Thomas, is that all you are taking to the conference?"

He laughed and gestured behind him at the slim little briefcase on the back seat, "Oh yes, I have everything I need in there."

The weather in Asheville turned out to be rainy and cold and everyone was concerned for Thomas' health as he moved from building to building without a coat or hat, though he never seemed to notice. At eighty-eight, he shepherded the conference along, led sessions, signed books, met with friends from early morning until late at night. On one memorable evening he presented a rousing poetry reading accompanied by bassist Eliot Wadopian in which Thomas invited the entire audience to join in!

On the way home, driving through the rain, I thought that Thomas would be exhausted. Instead he suggested we stop for dinner at a snug little restaurant in Winston-Salem to have a glass of wine and talk about the conference.

After ordering our meal, I commented that I was grateful for the depth of soul he had brought to the conference. He responded with a strength that amazed me: "Descartes took the soul out of the universe and I am determined to bring it back in." Thus began an animated conversation about the soul.

Expanding on his remark, Thomas acknowledged the work of Carl Jung who, he said, built a bridge to the soul by discovering that our genetic coding has both psychic and physical dimensions. "The universe has soul in all its living dimensions," Thomas said. "The psychic and the physical are two distinctive aspects of everything living—different, but not separable. One does not negate the other and neither can be substituted for the other. Each brings a distinctive way of knowing, and the universe nourishes both."

I could see that Thomas, despite whatever fatigue he may have felt, was on to a subject that was foundational in his thinking and I fumbled in my purse for my notebook. Without missing a beat, Thomas slid his cocktail napkin across the table for me to write on as he expanded on his topic.

"There is an animating principle of soul that is invisible and hidden in every living thing. It is the soul that constitutes us as persons. The psyche or soul, is primary, the essential component of life, but everything not scientific is considered unreal or without substance. In structuring the thought of the modern world, René Descartes established mind and matter and wiped out the soul of the world.

"Birds and plants were just seen as mechanisms without any vital principles. The earth became a resource to be used rather than a presence to be communed with as in the Chinese and American Indian understanding of the earth as an abiding world, a real world."

Thomas seemed to be saying that in the evolution of consciousness, an understanding of the soul force that connects all creatures, human and non-human, had been denied, which brought about a separation between humans and the natural world. When I asked if I was understanding him correctly, he nodded and added, "The perception of the Divine became historical, that is, in the past. The emphasis was on the linear and the literal rather than on the cosmological and the cyclical. Humans, who had formerly seen themselves as a 'ritual insertion' into the cosmos, lost their soul sense of integration with the cosmological order. The natural world and the human world, two dimensions of mystical rapport, were separated." He paused for what seemed like a very long time before he spoke again. "Psychically we cannot endure living on earth without a sacred context."

Thomas went on to speak with quiet clarity and great depth about how the feeling for reality in its depths had been lost in the past centuries of scientific analysis and technological manipulation of the earth. Because of this, he said, the symbolic world with its sacred qualities was lost and the earth assaulted.

"We gave away our subjectivity, our very souls to the objective reasoning mind," he said. "You might say we conspired in our own diminishment in agreeing to live a divided life when interiority, or subjectivity, got lost in the process of 'progress.'

"Subjectivity, also called 'consciousness,' is the interior numinous component present in all reality. Communion is the ability to relate to all other species, due to the presence of subjectivity and differentiation. Together these create the grounds for the inner attraction of things for one another. The removal of the soul began with the mechanistic trend of the modern world which has led to the loneliness of living in a world where the sacred has been banished."

As I sat there listening to Thomas speak of the tragic loss of soul through the centuries, I seemed to feel it viscerally. Outside the rains beat down on the roof of the restaurant with renewed force.

We sat without speaking for some time before I asked him how we could begin to recover ourselves.

When Thomas finally answered, it was to say, "There is a soul-loss that comes with the elimination of the greater context of the surrounding world. There is no inner life without outer experience. To not see the stars diminishes us and diminishes them. The spiritual dimension of the universe must be recognized as well as the physical. We restore ourselves through our awareness. We see the beauty, wonder and intimacy of the natural world through the soul, and we each come to our own distinctive ways of knowing. 'To be' is to be qualitatively different. There is a special quality of the universe that is unique in every individual. The soul awakens to a universe that aims at immense diversity, diversity within unity. Difference would have no meaning without unity.

"We must resist the effort to reduce to sameness. In sameness we can't give to each other. In our differences, soul intimacy makes us constantly exciting to one another. As humans, we have the soul capacity to develop understanding relationships with one another and intimacy with the natural world.

"Soul gives us our entrancement with the natural world's beauty, wonder and intimacy. We can experience a sense of the sacred through our unique soul consciousness that gives us insight and understanding. It is the soul that leads us to the greater context of our lives and allows us to behold the Divine in the universe through creation. We have to awaken specific human faculties in our deeper capacities; we have more profound dimensions than we realize. We need to develop qualitatively by recognizing the spiritual characteristics of the human soul."

Thomas had so developed an integral understanding of the universe that every thought was whole and part of a whole at the same time. "The universe," he continued, "is the natural context of the Divine but is distinct from it; we need to realize the Divine as the origin and destiny of the universe. The natural world is that which bears a mysterious presence that we refer to as the Divine that we feel through our souls—in the dawn, the sunset, the movement of the tides, the emergence of living forms. In those transformational moments in which we become aware of them, the comprehensive and the particular come together, you might say; the whole of the universe and the whole manifesting in each aspect of it are brought together through the individual soul who fulfills it. The task in shaping a new future calls upon us to be in union, not just with our rational faculty, but also with the deeper structures of the reality of the soul that allows us to be truly present to the natural world. Subjective communion with the earth overcomes its analytical, mechanistic aspects."

Then just as our food was being served, Thomas completed his thoughts: "The work now is in the realm of immanence. What is being lost today in western civilization is the development of soul capacities, which can lead us to our primary source of understanding within the mind, the imagination, and the emotions. The human-earth relationship can teach us to recover these through our unique human ability to reflect on the magnificence of a sunrise, the miracle of a humming bird, the profusion of blossoming flowers, the awesome sight of a waterfall, the lightning and thunder of the great storms. Through these outer experiences come our inner development and our creativity. There is a certain presence of the Divine that is felt that must be practiced over time to establish unity; this sense of the sacred is the aim of the soul in a lifetime."

When dinner was over, we drove back to the Hermitage in silence.

❀ ❀ ❀ ❀ ❀ ❀

A few days later I took a walk on the land at Timberlake with my notebook under my arm. I sat down on an old hollow log alongside the pond and wrote, "The psychic and the physical ... two distinctive aspects of who we are as living forms ... the inner and the outer, two realities that we live in simultareously, each different, but not separate. Neither can be substituted for the other; each brings a distinctive way of knowing."

The old maple tree hanging over the pond could certainly be described in quantitative ways by its height or its circumference, but it could also be expressed as a particular presence that protects the "Wishing Rock" below it, which children who visit here love so much.

The first way of seeing with the physical eye shows a world of fact. The second seeing is a beholding with the eye of the soul that reveals a world of meaning. With the second there is an inner deepening of our relationship with the tree.

"As I become more still," I wrote, "I breathe into the golden color of the maple leaves, into its shape as it leans over the pond, into the beauty, wonder and intimacy of the moment ... "

A breeze stirred the air, the sun shone through the trees all around, a fish moved in the water creating concentric circles on the surface of the pond. In that moment I could feel the "communion of subjects" of which we are all a part.

I remembered what Thomas had said about the universe nourishing both the psychic and the physical; both are connected to the soul of the universe. I saw that he was giving us a glimpse of another world in this world that had at its heart what he had called "the interior binding force of the universe" from his Confucian studies. He was helping us to see, to feel, to penetrate below the surface of life and to dwell in its depths.

He was helping us recover our souls.

Chapter Seven

The Hermitage and Intuition

It was several weeks before I felt that I had even begun to integrate the deep conversation on soul through my daily reflections and walks in the woods. I knew only that Thomas' understanding had spoken to some questions I had been carrying inwardly all my life and I was eager to ask him more about them. I finally called and we made a date to talk.

It was a languid fall afternoon as I drove to Thomas' modest dwelling on the outskirts of Greensboro; I had been there before but had never paid close attention to the surroundings until that day. One of his nieces had remodeled an old stable on her land when Thomas decided to return to North Carolina after his years at the Riverdale Center in New York. He moved in contentedly and named his new abode "The Hermitage."

To reach his place one had to drive over a slightly unstable bridge, turn right off Four Farms Road onto a gravel drive, which twisted and turned past a lake, and then park opposite an open field under an old oak tree reminiscent of his favorite red oak at the Riverdale Center.

As I parked my car and walked up the thirteen carpeted steps that led to Thomas' apartment, I remember my quiet anticipation, thinking that the day held a kind of grace.

He greeted me with a cheerful, "Come in, come in, how's everything out your way?" and told me to look around while he made us each a cup of tea. His place was simply furnished with a couch, a large chair, a coffee table, and a dining table stacked with papers and books above which hung an assortment of framed awards along with an array of dried leaves Thomas had collected on his walks.

Around the doorframe to his study I noticed a large number of Post-it notes with numbers and messages on them, and I called out to ask him what they were for. He responded with a chuckle, "Oh, they are reminders of things I have to do!"

I said, "How do you know which one to tackle first?"

He grinned and said, "I just close my eyes and pick one!"

He brought the tea into the living room and placed it on the coffee table and we sat down together on the couch. "Now," he said, "how's yourself?"

I explained that I had several journal entries on soul that I wanted to read to him. He settled back to listen, and when I was done, he provided a thoughtful and measured response: "We have the capacity to awaken to the inner life of things. It is about another way of knowing, an 'origin-al' way of knowing, you might say. It is a knowing that is connected as a tendril of the heart to the heart of the universe. It is a numinous awareness, an intuitive consciousness, a second voice, that resides beneath the rational faculties and is actually the approach to transformation."

As usual, I waited while he paused before enlarging upon his topic. When he went on, I again felt the depth and breadth of the Asian influences that he had integrated so deeply into his own thinking.

"The ancient Chinese had a definition of man as the *hsin* of heaven and earth," Thomas continued. "The word itself is written as a pictograph of the human heart. It means that 'man is the understanding heart of heaven and earth' or 'man is the psyche or the soul of the universe.' We are now awakening to the inner life of the heart in the human and the heart in the interior life of the universe."

By this time, Thomas was standing up and fully into his subject. To my great chagrin, I had run out of paper in my small notebook. Thomas noticed, walked over to his dining table, picked up a notepad and handed it to me while continuing to speak.

"Now, as we said before, the universe has soul in all its living dimensions; every creature has a deep psychic life, an intuitive connection to the Divine that was lost when our perception of the Divine became historical rather than immediate.

"Through the new story of the universe that we now acknowledge to be both physical and spiritual, we are beginning to see through new eyes, through a new, yet very old intuitive awareness that has been lost and is now being recovered. We are recovering an inner way of knowing which is a way of being that is desperately needed at this time when we can no longer bear the loss of the sacred within ourselves and within the earth. It is a distinctive way of knowing, separate from science; the two do not negate each other but they are not the same.

"In science, thought is organized around separateness and differences, parts are dissected, analysis and judgment prevail; with intuition, thought leads to synthesis and vision. We need both kinds of awareness, the inspiration of the intuitive and the critical faculty of the scientific intelligence, but science has been overdone in reference to the intuitive consciousness. Only through intuition can we experience a sense of the sacred.

"You can't understand the universe simply through science— it is one way of knowing directed toward analysis and use. The intuition is another way of knowing through the heart—the song of the birds, the sky at night, the magnificence of mountains and seas.

"You can see a forest at twilight with its changing light forms and appreciate it without knowing its science; you are experiencing 'another way of knowing' as you do. Our gesture toward the universe should be toward one of supplication for greater understanding through this other way of knowing that is really beyond words. In these present moments we actually discover our transformative nature."

I remembered reading an interview that Thomas had with poet Thomas Rain Crowe in 1990 in which Thomas had said: "I am constantly in an aware, analytical frame of mind, but also simultaneously, in a dream state of mind. We need both kinds of awareness. But the more we can function out of the immediacy of our arational responses, the better off we will be."

When I quoted this to Thomas, he nodded and replied, "With rationality we are never completely satisfied. Expansion of rationality is different from the expansion of intuition, which can bring a depth of understanding and a sense of the sacred."

Thomas paused then and sat down briefly to collect his thoughts and determine how to continue. I waited with great anticipation, feeling that with the strength of his comments he had moved again into what was deeply foundational in his thinking. He sipped his tea briefly before going on.

"Intuition is the unique quality of the human that is also the consciousness of the earth and the eventuality of the universe because it can reflect on the reality of the universe, its origin and its history. You might say that intuition is the foundation of reason that is laid down first in a child before the rational faculties are added on like grace notes." He smiled, pleased at how his words had come out in the immediacy of the moment.

"Every child carries this deep intuition but then loses it within a culture that doesn't understand or honor the intuition. It can remain lost forever. When the Chinese philosopher Mencius spoke of the need for recovering the heart of the child in later life, he was speaking of this inner knowing that we are talking about which is our *real* authentic nature and the goal of all our searching. Once rediscovered and *practiced*," he put great emphasis here on "practiced," "this 'indwelling' can give amazing value to our lives in the midst of all we experience.

"The natural world activates the intuition in the mind— what we *see* in the rocks and trees and flowers—and from this we very gradually begin to *see* the whole universe as a manifestation of the Divine. The comprehensive and the particular come together, as I like to say. Everything and everyone can be *seen* as both whole and part of the whole of the entire universe, and a sense of the sacred—" (here Thomas waited for the right word to come to him, and when it did, it was the same word he used when we first spoke about a sense of the sacred) "*affixes*—a sense of the sacred *affixes* itself within us in response to the natural world. We are able to ground ourselves in our own experience and reclaim our inner subjective knowing. As we add to our inner knowledge, we become more conscious of what was there originally. It is a healing both for ourselves and for the earth, for only a sense of the sacred can save us."

"Thomas," I asked him, "how do we recover our intuitive awareness?"

"It is an emerging process we are talking about," he said. "There is a great need to understand the sequence of universal emergence—the shaping of the galaxies, the shaping of the earth, and the refined shaping of human consciousness. This story is our personal story. We begin where the universe begins. Our souls, as well as our bodies, began to be shaped at that time. From the beginning, the universe has been spiritual as well as physical. From the beginning there has been, on a universal scale, a psychic and spiritual as well as a material process unfolding and developing.

"In past centuries the intuitive and visionary dimensions of the universe have been omitted in favor of the mechanistic and that has been tragic. Today these are emerging again as part of the evolutionary process and we can recover them if we can learn to see and work in the realm of immanence, for our real hope lies in the inner dynamics of our own nature. We must learn to recognize the promptings that emerge from our own depths."

We sat silently for a long time as we both contemplated the enormity of the words that had come to him.

I finally asked, "Thomas, are you saying that in this present time, for our survival and the survival of the planet, that we must be about recovering this intuitive awareness, this interior, inner soul dimension that has been lost?"

When he replied, he repeated the words he had used in our earlier discussion about relationships: "We are being changed. We are being adjusted to see everything in its true proportion. We are being driven down to the heart with its radical interior tendencies."

Thomas stood up then and said: "Come back next week and we'll talk more about this in regards to children."

❀ ❀ ❀ ❀ ❀ ❀

It was several days before I could resume my walks in the woods, so powerful was my last visit with Thomas that I needed time in stillness to absorb his words. When I did go out, I seemed to see all things in a new light: the way one fallen tree was held in the embrace of another, the overhead flight of a red-shouldered hawk, a flotilla of geese making a six-point landing on the dark waters of the pond, everything announcing itself in the "family of things," as the poet Mary Oliver has written.

"To be in rapport with the uniqueness of things," as Thomas had said, and yet to see that, "everything is bonded to everything

else," helped me see how the natural world could activate a sense of the sacred. I began to see with my inner intuitive eye that the natural world was teaching what I needed to learn ... patience from the enduring qualities of the oak trees, gentleness from the tiniest forest plants, softness from the grove of loblolly pines. Change, transformation, it was all before me and I was part of it all.

I saw that I had always been in search of an outer reflection of what was within and that now in my moments in the woods I was finding it all around me in every living thing. I realized from within that there was indeed a psychic-spiritual inheritance ... a love of the earth that came to us through the ages from the universe that was in great danger of being lost in this time. I allowed myself to go deeply into the grief.

As if to bring consolation, the resident blue heron landed in the top of a close-by tree to tell me that the natural world was offering to help ... that the "mutual-enhancing relationship" between us was bringing us into a participatory experience with one another.

When one notices in a particular moment—the word "notice" comes from "to know" as in an inner way of knowing— a very special relationship comes into being. In that moment with the heron I felt a direct experience of the sacred and I knew that the natural world was trying to come to our aid, if we could only learn to listen to it and trust it.

And as part of the universe, if we could only learn to listen to our intuition, our soul's knowing, and really come to trust it, perhaps the human-earth reunion, so long overdue, could finally take place.

Chapter Eight

Children of the Twenty-First Century

Thomas Berry had a deep love for children, all children; they were always "closest to his heart" as he put it. In his compassionate dedication to *The Great Work* he wrote:

> To the children
> To all the children
> To the children who swim beneath
> The waves of the sea, to those who live in
> The soils of the Earth, to the children of the flowers
> In the meadows and the trees in the forest, to
> All those children who roam over the land
> And the winged ones who fly with the winds,
> To the human children too, that all the children
> May go together into the future in the full
> Diversity of their regional communities

Thomas had inspired us at every juncture in the development of the Center for Education, Imagination and the Natural World and was always keen to know how things were going.

When he proposed a time to talk about the children at our last conversation, I knew he would first want an update on our mission, "to bring into vision a new relationship between the inner life of the child and the beauty, wonder and intimacy of the universe."

I also knew that he would create an inner space on that day for me to share the evolution of the work with him, but I didn't know how it would happen. In all the years I met with Thomas he never asked for specifics about anything, but instead somehow opened up an "intimate communion of thought" that provided a context in which large thoughts could enter and find welcome.

On this particular winter afternoon, as I climbed up the thirteen carpeted steps to his Hermitage, I reflected on this with eager anticipation. One always felt better after a visit with Thomas, as if the cramped quarters of the ego could open up and out into the vast cathedral of the universe.

He was waiting for me and had two cups on the kitchen counter with tea bags in them. The water in the kettle was already hot.

"Sit down, sit down and tell me how's yourself and everyone out your way," he began as we carried our tea to the table in front of the couch and chair. I waited to see where he would begin and there was a long silence until I realized that Thomas was waiting for me, as if no time had passed since our last visit two weeks ago. I waited a bit longer to be sure that my hunch was correct and then began:

"Well, Thomas, I have recently had the joy of being with those who have not lost their spiritual vision and who participate freely in a real communion of subjects with trees, plants, animals and all living things of the earth. These visitors to Timberlake Earth Sanctuary who are giving us courage to keep going are between the ages of three and eight years old."

"Yeah?" he said softly with a smile.

"You know how we watch for those special magical moments at our Center that bring children into a direct personal connection with the natural world? Well, I've brought some of them to share with you."

Thomas settled himself into his chair to listen with full presence as I continued:

"A group of seven year olds stopping suddenly on their trail walk one windy fall day to carefully observe a tiny spider web tossing back and forth. They watched in silent amazement for several minutes as the spider worked to repair it.

"Three five year olds sitting in rapt attention observing the movement of tiny golden frogs in the creek near the Creeping Cedar Trail.

"A group of seven to ten year olds at our summer dance camp thoughtfully absorbing the shapes and rhythms of the earth and then creating collaborative dance and movement patterns from them which they performed among the trees.

"An incredible moment of intimacy on Timberlake Trail when a gray fox and a group of eight year olds, teachers and parents, unexpectedly came face to face. Each stood in absolute silence as they experienced an encounter of deep communion.

"And the response of a six year old girl after being asked to listen deeply to the sounds of the woods: 'I even heard the beating of my own heart,' she said."

When I finished, Thomas smiled in deep delight and began to speak very seriously. "The child is growing up today in a geo-biological moment that has never before happened in sixty-five million years. The life of the child has always been *organized* (and here Thomas paused to give the word emphasis), around a real abiding world of beauty, wonder and the intimacy of living processes—the wind, frogs, butterflies—not a manufactured electronic world of virtual reality.

"The child has a natural bond of intimacy with the natural world, a remarkable sense of identification with all living things. There is an ongoing common language between children and the earth; it is a language of living relationships between themselves and the trees, the wind, the birds, the flowers.

"Children need this deep personal connection with the natural world, first in their early years. If we observe them closely, we can see how they are instinctively attracted to profound experiences of the natural world. They are reflecting the primordial need that all humans have for it. The child's first response to the natural world is attraction, touch, taste. Out of these experiences they come to know something regarding the world, which becomes the basis for their thinking. Children are then able to name and understand the explanations of things. Their minds begin to make relationships. They need both the physical and the psychic-spiritual; the earth gives them both."

"Thomas," I said, "in our work we are finding that children are not getting what you are suggesting they need. The older ones may know something about global warming and climate change, but often we find they don't know the sound of a bullfrog or the smell of spring rain."

Thomas nodded, acknowledging the complexity of the child's experience in this time. "The child of the twenty-first century will live a very different life than the child of the twentieth century when the natural world had a certain integrity.

"Our children will live with eight to ten billion people in a culture which did not embed itself within a cosmology. Now we initiate our children into an economic order based on exploitation of the natural life systems of the planet as our schools work to incorporate children into the world of the greater society. We have dedicated our educational programs primarily to the pursuit of so-called 'useful' knowledge, not to knowledge as intimate presence and participation in the wonder and magnificence of the universe through which we find the meaning of our existence.

"To achieve this 'useful' attitude we must first make our children *un*feeling in their relationship with the natural world, whereas the child is *organized* (and he used the word again with strong emphasis) for feeling everything living. They need direct experience of the living earth; the world we manufacture is not living. Children need to relate to living processes because they have a natural 'friendship relation' with the natural world that needs to be cultivated."

"So, Thomas," I asked, "are you saying that by disassociating a child from the natural world we are actually denying what is natural for them?"

Thomas nodded and said that without the natural world children are deprived of their *inner intuitive identities* and are starved for it in their minds and soul capacities. "The kind of knowing that comes from a relationship with the natural world is a way of being that is the foundational work for laying down enduring value and meaning, beauty and wonder. It is the very basis of music and poetry."

Slowly and thoughtfully he continued after a long pause: "The long-term survival of our children will actually depend on a new relationship between the natural and the human worlds. Children need to develop within a whole cosmology of the sun, moon, stars; they need to experience mystical moments of dawn and sunset. They need to awaken to a world to *relate* to as a communion of subjects, not to *use* as a collection of objects. Relationships are the primary context of existence, and children need to see us practice a *sympathetic presence* to the earth as a means for being in a mutually enhancing relationship to it.

"Parents need to say to the child, 'Let's go out into the sunset, let's go wade in the creek, let's go meet the trees.' Children need to breathe, to inhale with the beauty, wonder and intimacy of the whole earth. A sense of the sacred begins here. As children learn to understand the sacred nature of the universe from adults they will reproduce that sacredness in their lives in individual ways."

"And if they don't have that exposure to the natural world?" I asked him.

"The attraction cannot be eliminated," he replied, "there will always be a sense of unfulfillment."

"How then should we address the needs of children in our educational programs?"

Thomas paused for a moment and his thoughtful response reflected his deep concern for children and the future of our planet: "The child needs to be initiated into feeling at one with the universe through both inner and outer development. The universe story connected with earth studies is now presented only in its physical aspect; it must also have a spiritual dimension to initiate the child into a deeper relationship with the natural world in order to evoke the numinous and mysterious aspects that a child needs for entrancement with life.

"Our most basic issue is how we bond with the earth. Every field of education needs to be integrated into the new sacred story from geology, biology and astronomy, to poetry, literature and the arts. *Both* the scientific and the spiritual story are needed for children to become intimate members of the earth community."

Thomas paused for a moment, which gave me an opportunity to ask him to say more about the importance of story.

"The child brings a fresh participation in the world that contains story," he said. "Story is the result of imagination and wonder that carries the mind beyond reason into the world of the infinite. The language of the imagination carries humans into a greater depth of understanding of a world of beauty, wonder and intimacy that has a realism far beyond data and measurement. There is an outer and an inner world, which need to be nourished together, which is why both stories, the scientific and the spiritual, need to be told.

"But the order is important. Children need to learn to laugh and play and sing before they know how to develop a scientific understanding. It is the delight in nature we tend to lose through science. With science we receive the mechanics of things but lose the deeper meaning. Education in the twenty-first century should be about knowledge as understanding and knowledge as presence through which children and young people can find the meaning of their existence and their interrelatedness with all living forms. They need to develop interiority, a sense of wonder at the amazing differentiation in the universe, a sense of relationships, imagination, and the feeling of belonging to the whole universe.

"We must awaken a capacity in the child to go into the universe and then into the human world to be present to others. Children come from the spiritual world and have this consciousness; we need to give them confidence in it."

Thomas then returned to the work our Center was doing with children: "All that you are doing gives children a sense of belonging and meaning. Children of today need to know they belong where they are in a time when they are losing their self-orientation and ritual meaning. You are giving them another way of knowing, an 'origin-al' intuitive way that we have spoken of before. You are affirming their consciousness by giving them a context for their own experiences. A child is diminished when so much is given from the outside instead of being evoked from the inside."

I told Thomas how we were drawing parallels between the life processes of the creatures and trees and plants and the children themselves in such a way that they could see that everything and everyone is always transforming. I told him how we were giving children an opportunity to express their experiences in the natural world through art and writing and dance in a continuing sequence of transformations.

"Children need the magic idea of creation all life long," Thomas said. "And they can find themselves, their own uniqueness as part of it all, along with the frog and the butterfly and the flower in one single earth community. As they grow to understand their belonging within this larger context, their natural longing to create a better world will increase and they can learn new ways of functioning and creating within a sustainable life context. We need to continue to move into the twenty-first century knowing that within it the plight of the earth will be determined.

"Children need to see our efforts to preserve and appreciate the natural world as this can provide them with a main concern as they grow into adulthood. And," he added, repeating what he had told me at the bagel shop, "they can learn *appreciation* as a key to all knowledge because it constitutes an approach to everything."

I realized that the conversation was coming to an end when Thomas stood up and said, "What needs to be restored to children is, fundamentally, the universe. We want our children to experience a new dawning."

Thomas then disappeared into his small study and returned with several green bookmarks. Printed on them was his poem, "It Takes A Universe," which he proceeded to read aloud with great gusto:

The child awakens to a universe,
the mind of a child
to a world of wonder
Imagination to a world of beauty
Emotions to a world of intimacy
It takes a universe to make a child
Both in outer form and inner spirit
It takes a universe to fulfill a child
And the first obligation of each generation
Is to bring the two together
So that the child is fulfilled in the universe
And the universe is fulfilled in the child
While the stars ring out in the heavens!

Thomas sat down after his dramatic reading and we both sipped tea in silence and deep mutual reflection about the children and the world that will await them in the future.

❋　❋　❋　❋　❋　❋

I left Thomas that day with mixed feelings ... I knew that all he had said was deeply true from our experiences in connecting children with the natural world, but I also felt a heavy heart in knowing that the deeper significance of that relationship for children and for the future of the earth was not being recognized to any extent in educational institutions.

That night I had a dream of a pre-dawn moment and these words were with me when I awakened:

Deep darkness enfolds us ... we who walk on two legs as well as those who walk on four as well as those who burrow in the soil, fly with wings, swim in the waters ... all connected like tendrils to the heart of the universe ... united within its holy mystery ... but separated from one another by the abyss that the mind has created.

We wait in this moment ... being changed as we do ... adjusted, transformed by the darkness in which we wait ... We wait in silence with the universe breathing through us, waiting in radical trust for the dawning that will bring a new light of understanding that we are a communion of subjects, part of one single earth community that will live or die together.

Still waiting, still silent, we gradually, gradually become aware of hearing the echo of the Powerful Loving Voice that has spoken through every cosmic activity since time began.

We begin to feel a new heart-force within and around us, a new energy birthing ... Through roots of trees, stirrings of tiny wings, winds beginning to move, darkness begins to yield to the light of the sun's gradual presence ...

Skies now turn from darkness to gradual light; white to brilliant orange and pink streaks framing the sun's emergence in holy majesty ... and all we of all species, human and non-human who have huddled together in darkness, all we who stand, walk, crawl, fly and swim, stretch upward to receive the blessing of our emergence into a new dawn.

Chapter Nine

Presence and Identity

It was late November and the trees, now bereft of leaves, were beginning to show their anatomy. Seen from the other side of the pond they looked like India ink outlines in the gathering dusk.

I had been invited to speak at a conference at Camp New Hope "down the road a piece," as we say in the South, and discovered that Thomas was also on the program that weekend. I called to ask if he wanted a ride but he said he would be taking his own car.

He arrived before I did on that Friday afternoon and when I drove up, he came over to ask if he could help me unload. I told him I would do it later and we walked up to the lodge together for dinner and the evening program.

When the evening was over I looked around for Thomas. Not finding him, I walked down to the cabin where I had been assigned and to my amazement, found all of my belongings laid out in the room. My sleeping bag had even been carefully unrolled on one of the cots.

The next morning I ran into Thomas at breakfast. "Did you see the sunrise this morning?" he asked cheerfully. "I placed your sleeping bag facing east!"

Arising on the final morning of the conference, I could see the day was looking ominously like snow. As I approached the lodge I encountered a group of people gathered outside performing a circle ritual. Thomas was gaily taking part without a jacket or hat to everyone's consternation. Someone went into the lodge and returned with a too-large coat and a woolen cap and proceeded to thrust them on him as he continued good-humoredly to move around the circle.

Afterward in the kitchen, the conversation was about who would see that Thomas made it home safely in what was now a steady snowfall. Thomas spied me and said, "Carolyn will see me home," to which I readily agreed.

When we headed out, Thomas in his car and I in mine, we travelled west on Interstate 40 towards Greensboro. He took a fast lead and to my surprise turned off at the exit to Timberlake instead of heading onward to his Hermitage. I followed him to my own driveway where he stopped and got out of the car saying mischievously, "Well, I got you home safely!"

I replied that it was my understanding that I was to lead *him* home and he grinned in delight! I asked him to come in and have a bite to eat and he agreed. I made sandwiches and a pot of coffee and built a little fire in the fireplace as the snow continued to fall outside. Thomas didn't seem unnerved by the weather conditions and we settled in for what was to be another remarkable conversation, this time on the subject of identity and presence.

It began when he started to speak about his years at the Passionist monastery in New York where he said daily life consisted of silence, key moments and meditation. Thomas went on to say that "being practical, we lose the quiet contemplative dimension of life and don't nourish our souls, which makes us inadequate to the stresses of life."

Thomas described celebrating moments of dawn and sunset, solstice and equinox in a "Great Liturgy" of the cosmological order. "The human project," he asserted, "is validated by participation in the natural order. Our job as humans is to be part of the great hymn of praise that is existence."

He described attending prayer services with the other monks in the late hours of the night, then staying up to study until morning. When I asked him what question he was carrying in that study time, he paused as usual and then replied, "I was searching for a more universal vision." He then went on to say that in those years he had "found himself," which deeply interested me, and I asked him to speak more about identity.

"Identity is about communion," he began. "There is an attraction between the Great Self and the small self, the universe being the Great Self and the source of our inspiration and fulfillment. Communion is a process whereby a person discovers his greater Self, not within the limitations of his own individual being, but in relationship with others with whom he shares the same Divine Source and the same home on earth. Self identity and presence are eventually one."

I had to ask him to give me time to take that in. I had to continually remind myself that when Thomas spoke of relationships with others, he was referring not just to human relationships, but to relationships with all living forms. He had enlarged and compressed knowledge so deeply that it often took me considerable time to absorb the thoughts before I could continue to follow his train of thought. Thomas understood this and waited patiently until I was ready to continue.

"As you remember," Thomas resumed, "communion is the ability to relate to other species because of the deep interior practice of subjectivity and the deep outward practice of presence to the vast differentiation of the universe. By so doing, the grounds are created for the inner attraction of all things to each other. We actually activate the sacred dimension of the universe as we have discussed before. We become aware of the unity within the universe itself and within each of its components, and the intimate presence of each component of the universe with other components forming an actual communion of all things with one another."

"And the wonder is the feeling that we are actually part of it all?" I asked.

Thomas nodded. "We are part of the great community of life on earth evolving now from a context of personal identity to a sense of identity with an emergent universe. Only in the context of an emergent universe will the human project come to an integral understanding of itself. Something greater than our individual identity draws us on, something dim and uncertain, radiant with meaning. We have our personal identity, social identity, political identity, cultural identity, and now an earth identity and a cosmic identity. Everything exists in multiple dimensions. As we practice a presence to the natural world through our intuition we come to know ourselves, not simply as physical beings, but as spiritual beings as well, two dimensions of the same thing.

"We humans are modes of Divine presence who have forgotten our identity with creation. The practice of remembering gives us a sense of identity that keeps us integral with ourselves and with the universe, and can steady us in stillness in this historic period of dissolution and disintegration."

As I listened, I could see that Thomas was giving us a new direction for human evolution and I asked him to confirm this.

He responded by saying that we were now at a cultural impasse and that our responsibility in the light of our times was to give our cultural coding new expression. "The mission of our times is to reinvent what it means to be human. Intuition is the approach to transformation; analysis of parts is not our mission now. Parts only make sense when they come together. We are one earth community that lives or dies together.

"We are awakening now to the cosmic-earth-human process whereby all things have a genetic relationship with each other. We are discovering our place anew within the earth process. We depend on the earth to sustain us in body and soul. The earth becomes primary, the human derivative. We come into *relationship* to it instead of establishing an identity over and against it where the part is disconnected from the whole. We can only find ourselves through our relationship with the natural world. We shift from seeing the earth as a collection of objects for our *use* to seeing it as a communion of subjects in which we form one body with all living things. We begin to see ourselves as a species among species as earlier people did intuitively. Now we must do this deliberately. As we do so, we become more conscious of what was within us originally."

By this time I could see through the windows that the snow had enclosed the room in such a way that I had the image of being in one of those paperweights that you shake to create the illusion of a snowy winter scene. Only this was real, this conversation in my home on this day with the falling snow stacking up on the tall slanted windows, the crackling fire and my small dog napping beside us on a pillow. In the middle of it all was this remarkable man bringing his universal vision into the moment.

Thomas was deeply into his subject. "We discover our true identity, our presence within the universe in moments of communion in which we find true fulfillment." He stopped here to repeat again what he had shared with me at the bagel shop: "The entire evolutionary process depends on communion. Without this fulfillment that each being finds in beings outside itself, nothing would ever happen in the entire world. There would be no elements, no molecules, no life, no consciousness. The whole earth as a spiritual planet must become the basis for our identity. To be human is to be able to live in a spiritual-physical world, to see that every being is connected to every other being.

"The younger generation is growing up with a great need for a mutually enhancing relationship, a human presence to the earth. Young people need the greater identity beyond their own limited being which gives them a sense of belonging, a self-orientation, a sense of meaning and purpose in these times of great mobility and change. We all seek the expansion of our being which is why we are drawn so powerfully to the experience of the earth."

We both sat quietly after that to allow the truth of his words to penetrate into the moment.

Thomas finally broke the silence. "We are living in a period of transition, a period of 'groping' toward an uncertain future, which is asking those who are willing to move forward even when it can't be clearly understood where we are going. It is a new dynamic in history. Encouragement is needed to trust the unknowable future, to grope toward it, knowing that the universe is always expanding into greater and greater differentiation and deepening spontaneity, which produces evermore intimate self-bonding of its component parts and allows each individual to become evermore itself. Each one of us is a unique expression of the universe with our special intelligence, emotions and imagination. We are integral with the universe, not separate from it. The human is always validated by the relationship with the earth with differences fulfilled within unity."

"Thomas," I said, "you are returning us to our deeper soul identities aren't you? In forgetting the earth, we have forgotten who we are. Now you are helping us evolve toward Love as 'an inner presence to all things,' as you told me once before."

"Love is foundational," he replied, "and must continue to go forth and create a new century in the direction of compassion for the earth. That's why we all must participate now in the repair of our planet. We'll discover our identities as we

grow in the same Divine direction through our communion."
He then smiled, which I had come to understand meant the
end of the conversation.

Thomas stood up to leave. Though I protested about the
winter weather and unsafe highway conditions, he headed for
the door undaunted. Making his way to the car, which was
now completely covered by snow, he brushed off the windshield, started up the engine and slowly traveled down the
driveway until he was out of sight.

Soon I began receiving phone calls from worried Berry
family members concerned about Thomas' whereabouts. When
I explained Thomas' resolve to head home, they admitted having
similar experiences with his unwavering determination.

Several hours later the phone rang. "Carolyn, this is Thomas.
I'm home safe."

🐢 🐢 🐢 🐢 🐢 🐢

*I realized that evening that through each conversation Thomas
and I were having, he was adding yet another layer of understanding to my shift in consciousness. Here in this conversation
about identity and presence, I could see that in forgetting our
relationship with the natural world we were also forgetting our
relationship with the universe, the Divine, one another, and our
own souls.*

*Thomas was calling us to a new sensitivity that went beyond
aesthetic appreciation of the natural world to a deeper level of seeing
and being in relationship with it.*

Each day on my walks in the woods I practiced trying to remember my relationship with the natural world as I encountered amazing moments of presence: a tiny group of speckled bluebird eggs, the sound of a barred owl, a turtle laying her eggs in the middle of a walking trail. From these intimate moments and many others, I became aware of the "communion of subjects" of which Thomas spoke; I began to feel an identification with the whole. I began to see for myself the deep truth that he was communicating: when we learn to see the natural world as sacred, reciprocity begins to develop between the natural world and ourselves in a mutually enhancing relationship. In those stopping places, those moments of communion, I felt myself embedded in a sacred universe in which all opposites were reconciled. I had the feeling of being "home safe" within the great community of life.

"Love is an inner presence to all things," Thomas had said without further elaboration, saying only that love, given us in "germinal form" as Tielhard described it, "must be cultivated."

He had spoken of interior communion as "contemplation whereby one sinks deep into the subjectivity of one's own being to experience the totality of things." To experience the totality of things in interior communion meant for me, that I was to undertake a departure from my accustomed prayer life and journey inward to find reconnection with the Source of a universe that for billions of years has continued to create the conditions for life on earth. That journey would move me down past the chatter of the conditioned mind, the judgment of the intellect, the lists of endless tasks, the sympathies and antipathies of the personality, the distractions of technological fascinations, the fears and re-

sentments of the dark subconscious, the bondage of the past, the heavy cultural overlay of the present historic period.

In that very deep place I discovered the contemplative dimension, the interiority that is part of the nature of being human and the unifying dimension within us all. There in the depths of the psyche I discovered the inner valley of the heart where all was still and all was holy. Over a period of time, I discovered that Love itself was both the source and the goal of the immense sacred journey of the universe and of each individual. As the Creator of all things, it is both the universal origin and the destiny to which all return. Love is the inner place where the soul is truly home safe.

As Thomas said, "Love is foundational." In the midst of change, Love doesn't change. It is stable and also fluid. It goes forth as the impulse in every living thing to create. It brings us into communion with all living things, into mutual presence with one another. It brings us into trust in an unknown future, into gratitude for the sacredness of life itself.

We are now being called by the universe to bring Love forth as an inner presence to all things, to bring a dimension to the human-earth relationship that will enable humans and non-humans to live in a "mutually enhancing" way, to further life itself.

Thomas was returning us to our deeper identities ...

He was guiding us home.

Chapter Ten

Memories from the Later Years

In 2003, Thomas moved from his Hermitage to the Well-spring Retirement Center in Greensboro to take advantage of the care it could provide in his later years. He accepted the move cheerfully, leaving behind all his material possessions, including his many books and awards. He simply stepped out of one reality into another, saying, "We are always opening onto greater life."

He was no longer driving by this time, so I began to pick him up for lunch or dinner or special trips to Timberlake. We also had several little adventures over the next few years, which gave me additional insights into my great friend's special charm and sense of humor.

Outside one entrance of the retirement center was an overhang with benches for waiting residents. No matter the weather, Thomas was always there ahead of my arrival, sitting quietly in his favorite blue sweater. He would rise quickly as I drove up, and I would try to stop and run around to the passenger side to help him into the car. I seldom managed to reach the door before Thomas got to it, and we would then awkwardly negotiate getting him into the car and fastening his seat belt before I returned to the driver's side.

I remember always saying a little prayer as I drove out of the retirement center for the safe transport of this dear soul who was a treasure to so many all over the world.

We would drive along making small talk which neither of us really liked, but we also understood the need to wait until we got settled in at the Green Valley Grill before a more spacious in-depth conversation could take place. Once we arrived in the parking lot, Thomas would allow me to assist him out of the car and into the restaurant.

By this time in his life, Thomas had suffered a stroke and was struggling with complications from a shoulder injury, yet he never spoke of his infirmities. Occasionally he would forget a word he needed to complete a thought, and would sometimes pause and ask me to supply it. In those moments, I would say another quick prayer to offer the right word from our past conversations. Sometimes I succeeded; often I didn't, which never seemed to bother him. He would just wait and then continue expressing his thoughts when the correct word came to him.

Our lunch conversations would meander through history, lingering here and there as Thomas related stories that would bring new understanding to the evolution of the universe in its largest dimensions. Thomas saw through the centuries the weaving patterns of darkness and light, and always emphasized the purposefulness of life that had brought us through each crisis.

One day after a long lunch, we realized that the waitstaff had cleared all the tables and we were the last occupants in the restaurant. We hastened to finish our visit and as we stood up to leave, Thomas inadvertently knocked over his coffee cup, spilling a small amount on the table. Immediately three of the waitstaff showed up to "help" what must have seemed to them a doddering elderly couple. An uncomfortable moment hung in the air until Thomas smiled and said, "Carolyn and I always have a *fling* when we're out together." We all laughed and came into a new relationship with the moment and each other.

When I returned Thomas to the retirement center, he would leave my car and walk to the overhang where he always turned around and waved goodbye as I drove off.

❋ ❋ ❋ ❋ ❋ ❋

During one of our lunch dates in the spring of 2005, I had the pleasure of telling Thomas about the recent publication of a new book entitled, *Last Child in the Woods: Saving Our Children from Nature-Deficit Disorder.*

"Who wrote it?" he asked.

"His name is Richard Louv," I replied.

"That's wonderful," Thomas said in delight and said he wanted to meet the author who had accomplished such a task.

The opportunity came a few months later, when Rich Louv came to Raleigh for a book signing event. A few hours prior to the event, a reception was held that was cosponsored by Rich's publisher Algonquin Books and our Center for Education, Imagination and the Natural World. Friends brought Thomas to the reception from Greensboro.

I will never forget the joy I felt as I introduced the two men on that evening.

Thomas said to Rich, "A magnificent accomplishment!"

And Rich replied, "You have always been my hero!"

❀　❀　❀　❀　❀　❀

One day I received a call from the office of the Pro-Tem of the North Carolina Senate asking if I could bring Thomas Berry from Greensboro to attend a meeting at the state legislative building in Raleigh. I was told that Senator Marc Basnight, who was in charge of the North Carolina Senate at that time, had heard of Thomas' views on water conservation and was interested in learning more. I was informed very explicitly that the Senator's schedule was extremely busy and that he would have no more than twenty minutes to meet with Thomas. When I called Thomas to tell him of the invitation and the time limitations, he chuckled and said, "Sure, let's go!"

We set out early for an eleven o'clock meeting with Senator Basnight and were surprised to be met by a police escort as we entered the Raleigh city limits. As we drove toward the legislative building, Thomas asked me if I thought he should wear a tie to his meeting with the Senator. When I suggested that might be a good idea, Thomas pulled an aged and crumpled necktie out of his briefcase.

We were given a privileged parking space and then led to an elevator and up to a very large conference room that overlooked the city. At the appointed hour, Senator Basnight entered briskly and the conversation began. Twenty minutes passed, then forty, then an hour, then an hour and a half as the two men entered into a deep discussion about the state's water issues and then expanded, as so often happened in conversations with Thomas, to include the whole human-earth relationship.

Several people came into the conference room to remind the Senator of his other obligations, but each time they were told to wait. When the meeting finally ended, Senator Basnight thanked Thomas for his time. The conversation had lasted over two hours!

※　※　※　※　※　※

During his years at Wellspring, Thomas continued his conversations with people who came to visit him from all over the world. Even though he no longer could go to the airport to meet each one as he had done in prior years, he always welcomed them graciously to his small apartment.

"Relationships are the primary context of existence," he repeated often and he lived deeply into this value. This was especially evident when he talked about his family. Having returned to his birthplace, Thomas loved to engage with his large extended family. He delighted in describing the one hundred and thirty-five member Berry family reunions, and often shared poetry with me that he had written for various family members on special occasions such as birthdays, anniversaries and weddings.

❊ ❊ ❊ ❊ ❊ ❊

As the seasons passed, Thomas and I continued our long extended conversations on topics that engaged him. One in particular was about Thomas' views on *understanding*, which he said had been the "priority" of his whole life.

"In America," Thomas said, "the value has been on achieving knowledge that will be *useful*. The idea of knowledge as a means to achieve *understanding* and *fulfillment* has been secondary. I have sought a more complete understanding, a more profound understanding you might say. Understanding is the fulfillment of learning; learning itself is not the fulfillment. We can look back and see why we had to go through certain experiences in order to gain greater understanding. Once a person integrates knowledge, this is fulfillment.

"Knowledge can also lead to spiritual understanding. If one seeks understanding first, it leads to everything. The world of the infinite is not revealed completely in the finite world. We are led to continually seek. It is why God gives us our daily bread; it is why we have to keep on praying. It matters what we seek first; it does not come all at once. Love doesn't come to stay with just one kiss; it stays but in a limited way. Over time it gets better!"

Then Thomas added: "I also found a deepening of emotions necessary for a depth of understanding. That is where mind and perception come in. Appreciation comes in beyond that. The universe awakens us to our proper mode of understanding through our hearts as in the Eastern tradition where we hear, 'May my heart be awakened in this flower.'"

🦋 🦋 🦋 🦋 🦋 🦋

One December close to Christmas, Thomas handed me an envelope on which he had scrawled: "To Carolyn, Merrie Christmas."

Inside were written eight words:

Live fully,
Laugh often,
Forgive instantly,
Love always,
Thomas

🦋 🦋 🦋 🦋 🦋 🦋

When health issues required another move to the intensive care facility at Wellspring, Thomas chose a small monk-like room with a bath and a window overlooking a small garden.

I had a standing date with him every Thursday morning at ten o'clock when I would arrive and knock on his door. He would call out cheerily for me to come in, and I would open the door to see him seated in his leather recliner in front of the window. He always had a cream-colored American Indian blanket wrapped around his shoulders that seemed just right for the distinguished elder he had become.

Thomas was always glad to see me and would reach out his hand to touch mine with the same warmth and deep presence I had been privileged to know for so many years. Somehow there was never a student-teacher relationship with Thomas; he always treated me as a companion on the same evolutionary path. All that Thomas shared with me echoed his lived truth; it was never a description of moral right or wrong. His interest was always in our reconnection to the whole universe.

He would chuckle a bit each time I came, and always asked, "How's yourself, and what's going on out your way?"

I would give him an update on the activities of our Center and then he would say: "What question or reflection do you have for me today?"

We had only one hour now for our conversations and I tried to prepare in advance to use it wisely. I knew that he would enlarge upon anything I brought to him, so I tried to assess his strength before I asked him whether he preferred to speak about a specific question, such as the shift in consciousness from the conditioned mind to the heart, or to expound on a question we had touched upon in previous conversations. On some days he simply replied with a gesture that said it was my decision.

I always kept my journal with me to record his responses.

❀ ❀ ❀ ❀ ❀ ❀

By this time, I was going into the woods on most days to practice making the shift that allowed me to "see" everything around me through the new understanding that Thomas had brought into my life.

I would start with a meditation that would help me to move into the interior life, down below the surface of the mind where Love may be found. At first this took great effort, but over time it became easier with practice. From that place of inner stillness, I was able to behold through the eyes of the heart that the trees before me, the rocks, the twisted branches on the ground, the parchment leaves, and I myself, were part of the "numinous mystery from whence all things come." From this I would begin to feel the deep sense of the sacred of which Thomas spoke.

When I picked up a pinecone or a fallen leaf or a piece of quartz, I remembered anew that "we are touched by what we touch, shaped by what we shape, enhanced by what we enhance," as Thomas had put it. In the stillness of the woods, I could feel the reciprocity of a deepening relationship with the earth. I saw with new eyes that all living forms share the same mysterious life processes of gestation, birth, growth, development, death, and rebirth into new form. I saw that we were indeed "united in the Mystery" to which we all belong.

When I described my experiences in the woods to Thomas in his small room at Wellspring on Thursday mornings, he responded as he always did with an interpretation that expanded both mind and heart. "To behold is a particular mode of consciousness that brings us into our own identity and the universe into its own identity," he said. "You are finding your unity with the universe and discovering your fulfillment in these moments. This happens as you learn to see everything in the universe as a revelation of the Divine Mystery, the Source, from which it came into being.

"The natural world communicates Divine presence through all its creations; it is the meeting place for the Divine and the human to come together. There is the beauty, wonder and intimacy of things to each other, the 'indwelling,' that gives amazing value to our lives in the midst of it all."

* * * * * *

During one particular Thursday visit, our conversation turned to the aging process when Thomas remarked with characteristic good humor, "Life is taking a turn toward its 'late-stages.'"

I asked how this was affecting his life and he talked about fulfillment and his sense that his life had been an emotionally fulfilling experience. He was also pleased that he had been able to participate "somewhat" in the development of civilization.

"I've done a little bit, but not much," he said. "I have always tried to find the more perfect way. Teaching brings a person into greater diversity."

I asked him to say more about his own personal development.

"The sense of identity, I suppose you could say, is a major element in my own development," he replied.

"All your life you have been so advanced in your thinking," I said. "Did that create loneliness for you?"

"The more liberated I became, the freer and more authentic I felt, not imitative and approved," he responded. "I had to be myself. The main capacity I developed was the right to be different and the appropriateness of being different, which is a real challenge for young people. It was done as something of a protection and as an assertion of identity."

"And your books, your writings—they were an expression of your identity?"

Thomas nodded. "I have been able to stay the course of my own thinking," he said firmly with deep conviction. "Through the stages of life, life becomes more comprehensible, becomes more integral. Knowing the natural world and knowing God becomes one knowing with two aspects as a person comes to know the Divine as manifest in the natural world."

I asked him if that knowing had deepened his connection with God and he replied, "My connection with God has never changed. It has only increased in clarity."

Thomas then went on to speak of the path of evolution, as he understood it in his later years. "Life normally moves to a period of spiritual development. A person has a need for physical, intellectual and spiritual fulfillment. It tends to become increasingly clear how these are related to each other. It is a most unique process in a time-development sequence, an unfoldment.

"As we grow older, we understand less and less rationally; the intuitive mind becomes greater and greater and the reasoning mind less and less. Appreciation increases."

"And what happens to people in the later stages of life who have not developed their intuitive capacities?" I asked him.

Thomas answered, "They have their own adaptations; everything turns to a deeper feeling. What we retain at the later stages is what we most deeply value and cherish. It has a lot to do with the quality of our relationships. Our first obligation is gratitude."

❋ ❋ ❋ ❋ ❋ ❋

Another day the subject of sainthood came up in our conversation.

"I hate piety," Thomas said. "If you 'saint' someone, you remove them from ordinary life and thus remove them from awareness. We are all part of the family of life on the same pilgrimage."

For Thomas Berry, who held strong opinions in this matter, we were all companions, none more exalted than any other.

❋ ❋ ❋ ❋ ❋ ❋

Even though my visits were briefer now, I came away from each conversation with renewed inspiration and commitment to continuing the practice of seeing anew. Thomas had so developed his heart and mind in the service of a sacred universe that it had become an immense interior temple in which he resided and which supported his life. I began to suspect the whole purpose of human striving might truly be to create this inner dwelling place for the soul, the *magnum opus* of our lives that Carl Jung spoke of, the individual "Great Work" to which Thomas Berry had addressed himself. I mentioned this to Thomas and he nodded in assent without comment.

❊ ❊ ❊ ❊ ❊ ❊

On another visit, I described to Thomas the beautiful dawns and sunsets I had observed at Timberlake Earth Sanctuary. This led us into a wonderful conversation about time.

"The dawn," said Thomas, "speaks of the celebration of new beginnings, the sunset of the supreme moment of continuity. At one time, the natural world and the human world were two dimensions of mystical rapport. The world was seen as a great cosmic ritual and humans were integral within it. Humans saw themselves as part of a cosmology, knew themselves as part of the whole cosmological order. Psychically, life on earth couldn't be endured without this. Everything had meaning.

"Everything and everyone was participating in the numinous, which gives meaning. Your experience of seeing the dawn and the sunset took you out of time, as we know it today. We have been taken out of our integral presence to the natural world, alienated from the universe by our participation in linear time only. We need to return to our experience of the human in the cosmological order. To recover cosmology is to recover a sense of the sacred in spacious moments in which time expands.

"The universe has a sequence of such moments in the celebration of dawn and sunset and in the very rhythm of the cosmos, but we have forgotten it," he continued. "The inner world of the soul needs to be activated by the experience of the outer world in all its grandeur. Our souls, our imaginations, our emotions, depend upon our immediate experience of the natural world. These moments wait for us to come into them. In present

moments, we begin to get the smell of home. Now we are beginning to develop energies for homecoming. Now we have the
smell of home. In these moments we sense the real world, the
abiding world."

Thomas concluded by saying that the "human project" is
now ready to receive the cosmos because of the desperation of
our situation in readjusting to planet Earth.

As I was leaving, he called out to say we could talk more
about time during our next visit.

I was deeply moved by this conversation and the possibilities it offered for our recovery of the soul and the sense
of the sacred. I began practicing moving consciously out of
linear time and into spacious moments that allowed time to
take in the natural world more fully.

I allowed my soul, my imagination, my emotions to be
activated by a patch of vivid green moss in the woods, the
texture of a cedar tree, ripples in the pond, birdsongs, breezes.
I would come to call this deep attention "soul time."

When I shared my notes with Thomas on my next visit, he
provided these thoughts: "The natural world is infused with the
presence of the Divine. As we enter into it in a state of receptivity
and courtesy, its sacred dimension reveals itself to us. Everything has this dimension with a certain identity and dignity to
be honored in a profound way. If we did this, we would not be
able to violate the integrity of the planet in any way."

As he spoke, I remembered the translucent moment on the
trail years earlier when Thomas held that tiny sprig of Creeping
Cedar in his hands. He had honored it in such a way that I felt

the presence of the Divine, the universe, and the earth come together. When I mentioned this to him, he replied by saying that out of the depths of our own souls we have our own unique experience of the universe. "Out of this," he said, "comes our re-enchantment with the earth."

I then reminded Thomas that he had promised to speak more about time and he responded by saying that we live in a "time-development sequence" that we must understand or we are doomed to repeat the mistakes of the past.

"We are organized to grow on in an ongoing creative universe that we are part of and that is calling us to heal and create as an integral part of it." The application and practice of this new understanding of time, Thomas explained, can lead us to the shift in consciousness that is called for at this time.

"We are here to remedy time. We remedy our understanding of the past by bringing it into the present, which reconciles it and heals it. The future should not be a rejection of the past, but its transformation."

With those words on that day, I felt the grace of redemption fill Thomas Berry's small monk-like room.

🐢 🐢 🐢 🐢 🐢 🐢

With every visit to Wellspring in those final years, I learned more about Thomas Berry's indomitable spirit. One Thursday morning when I arrived, Thomas was not in his room. As I went looking for him, I heard him call out to me from a small sitting room at the end of the hall. A member of the nursing staff had strapped a little device with bicycle pedals to his legs to improve his circulation and he told me quite cheerfully to sit down and wait for him to finish his "running."

"I'm getting ready to run a marathon," he said with a broad grin! I was touched that a man as highly independent as Thomas had been his whole life, could let go and let others help him. The whole staff at Wellspring loved his congenial nature and his willingness to let them care for him without resistance. He later told me, "Older people need to know they are being taken care of. I am learning so much in these later years."

Every time someone would ask him how he was doing, he would cheerfully reply, "I'm still in the game." The spirit always prevailed.

Though physically frail, Thomas was like a wick in a candle with nothing hiding his strong, transparent spirit. Speaking to me of his later years, he said, "Subjectivity, differentiation and communion have been of utmost importance to me. As we grow in complexity, there is a longing for greater simplicity. We become weary of endless descents and ascents and long for the middle ground of inner peace, the golden mean. In reconnecting with the universe, separation is overcome, as is dualistic thinking. The scientific joins with the mythic, space with time, the masculine with the feminine. A universal flow of thought becomes possible."

❀ ❀ ❀ ❀ ❀ ❀

Every day throughout his life, Thomas Berry continued to teach, revealing the consequences of human devastation to the earth, while at the same time always showing a way forward through a sense of the sacred that exists within every human soul.

On one of the last days of my visits, I told Thomas of seeing the incredible tiny being of a hummingbird that morning at my window and for a short time forgetting myself in a moment of wonder at its colorings, its featherings, its ability to balance itself and sip from the feeder. In that moment I felt a sense of the sacred that I wanted to share with him.

"You were allowing it to reveal the numinous presence that brings all things into being," he replied. "In that moment you knew the beauty, wonder and intimacy of the mystery we are united within."

"Thomas," I asked him, "are you saying that the inner sacred dimension of the human must have its correspondences in the outer world in order to be sustained?"

"The natural world activates the interior life," he said. "As the natural world diminishes in its splendor, so human life diminishes in its fulfillment of both the physical and spiritual aspects of our being.

"The inner spirit and the outer form are two distinctive aspects of a single mode of being. We find the presence of the Divine in every mode of created being and we discover a sacred mutuality with each. Humans and the earth have a mutual need for one another.

"It is this inner capacity for mutual presence that future generations must realize as they guide the course of human affairs in the twenty-first century. We are going through an exodus moment into an emergent universe; we are transitioning into maturity. We've not a clue what is ahead of us. We live in a universe that is contingent on us, not a universe that is determined in advance for us. We are giving up something to go into something strange and mysterious as we enter an entirely new era of the Ecozoic."

I asked him how we needed to prepare for this and then expressed my own concerns for future generations including my nine grandchildren.

He suggested that at our next meeting we should discuss what young people must understand as they go forward into their lives.

"We'll talk about the seeds of the future next time," he promised.

Chapter Eleven

Seeds of the Future

It was a week later in late May of 2009 that I headed to Wellspring for what was to be my last visit with my great companion. The sky was blue, the sun shining graciously, the earth breathing easily as I lifted the lock on the back gate to the retirement center. I moved into the hall and headed toward Thomas' room with great anticipation of what Thomas would say to future generations—"seeds of the future," he had called them.

In all my previous visits to Wellspring, Thomas had waited for me to ask him a question that would send him into the gulf stream of his deep mind, but this day was different. Today he had a very specific subject in mind.

He was sitting as usual in his recliner with his American Indian blanket wrapped around his shoulders. The spring sun streamed in upon him from the one window in the room. In the background I could hear the hum of activities in the building, but in Thomas' small room there was a sense of intimate enclosure, where a moment of considerable significance seemed to be gestating.

With my pen and notebook ready, I prayed that I could adequately take in what he was about to share with me as I felt a heightened urgency within him this morning. I could tell that Thomas had done much thinking in advance about the conversation we were about to have. But he still expressed his usual courtesy and hospitality by first asking, "What's going on out at your place?"

Then he turned to the subject at hand. "We need to talk about what to tell future generations, don't we?"

"Yes," I replied. "When our time was over last week, we were talking about our transition now into the Ecozoic Era. I asked you what can we tell succeeding generations, including my own nine grandchildren, about the way into the future and you said we would talk about it this week."

Thomas paused for a long time and finally began:

"Tell them something new is happening, a new vision, a new energy, a new sacred story is coming into being in the transition from one era to another.

"Tell them in the darkness of this time, a vast transformation is occurring in the depths of human consciousness, which is leading to the recovery of the soul, the earth, the universe and a sense of the sacred.

"Tell them that the Powerful Loving Voice that spoke through every cosmic activity is speaking again now through voices all over the earth—voices who recognize that loving the earth as their common origin unifies all. In the sacred, all opposites are reconciled.

"This Loving Voice is also speaking through every bird, leaf and star, and through the polar bear, the wolf and every threatened species, awakening humanity to see all living forms as a single sacred community that lives or dies together."

Thomas stopped to rest for a moment and then continued: "Tell them that the concern now must be for the preservation of the whole earth, a bio-spiritual planet; tell them that they must participate in mutual presence with the whole human venture in this perilous course of the future.

"Tell them that they must also develop the inner vision that we need if we are to make the adjustments required for a viable future. Our existential questions must now be: 'How do we relate to the earth and to the universe?' Our most basic issue is how we bond with the earth."

Then he added with a smile, "And tell them they will meet great companions along the way, including those that burrow in the soil, fly in the air and swim in the sea.

"Tell them that each of them has a unique part to play in this period of great transition and that each of them brings specialized emotions and imagination to this time and very different ways of knowing.

"Tell them that they can find their own story within the sacred story of the universe. Tell them that the journey of the universe is the journey of each one of them that can give meaning and purpose for their lives and guide them in the evolutionary process. Tell them to realize that the series of physical and psychic-spiritual transformations of the universe parallel their own individual transformations."

Thomas paused again and then said with particular emphases: "They can be helped going through their own difficulties by remembering the crises and transformations that the universe has survived and that they bear within themselves. Each crisis can bring about a higher level of consciousness. Tell them they can learn to deeply honor all processes of life, even the most difficult.

"Tell them to remember as they grope forward to create a new century of life in the twenty-first century, that the universe is still expanding and that they are part of that emergence as the direction of the universe moves always toward greater and greater life.

"Tell them that we live in a contingent, not a determinative universe; that we must create a new way of being as we transition from a period of devastating the earth to a mutually enhancing relationship with it.

"Tell them to seek their own role in the larger evolutionary process; tell them that humans are always in the process of *becoming*, always 'opening to greater life,' if they can learn to see it. Tell them the greatest need is to develop a sensitivity to recognize the inner promptings that emerge from the depths of one's own being where the sacred reality resides."

Here Thomas smiled. "We are all part of the family of humankind walking toward the light," he said.

"Above all, tell them to practice an intimate presence to the beauty and wonder of the natural world through their intuitive awareness that recognizes the oneness of all life; tell them to stop and enlarge moments throughout their days to become aware of the mysteries and miracles of creation all around them—the movement of a squirrel, the sound of a bird, the pattern of a leaf, changing patterns of light, the sun, the rain, the stars, dawn and sunset. Tell them we are not ourselves without everything and everyone else.

"Tell them to remember the great seasons and cycles of life. In moments of intimacy with the natural world they will recover the lost sense of the sacred in the human-earth relationship. And they will be participating in the evolution of a new consciousness on earth that can overcome the mental fixations of our times expressed in radical division between humans and the natural world. A mutually enhancing relationship will then become possible as the communion of all things is understood.

"Finally, tell them that it is of utmost importance that they become aware of the numinous sacred values that have been present in an expanding sequence over four and a half billion years of the earth's existence, and let them know that they will always be guided by 'the same Divine Power that spun the galaxies into space, lit the sun and brought the moon into orbit.'"

Thomas leaned back into his chair. Though exhausted, he smiled deeply knowing his task was complete.

As I leaned over to kiss his forehead, I knew that my task had just begun.

Our visit ended and I walked to the door. Before I left, I looked back for the last time at my dear companion. Thomas, despite his deep fatigue, was waving goodbye.

Chapter Twelve

Within the Cathedral

It was September 26th, 2009. The place was New York City. The occasion was the memorial service for Thomas Berry at the Cathedral of Saint John the Divine. Thomas had passed away four months earlier on June 1st.

I was grateful to be in New York. The summer had been filled with the emptiness of his absence.

The day was clear and cool with only a few scattered clouds moving behind the spires of the massive cathedral. Along with several others who were close to Thomas, I made my way up the hundreds of steps to the great entrance. Each of us was immersed in our own thoughts, each remembering our own special relationship to this man who had brought new human understanding to all who were ready to receive it, and who related to each one of us in a completely unique way.

My personal thoughts took me to that moment ten years earlier when I walked with Thomas on the Creeping Cedar Trail and began my own special journey with him.

Crossing over the threshold of the great open doorway, we made our way into the huge vestibule of the cathedral, past the burning prayer candles that had sustained pilgrims of the soul's journey for over one hundred years, and slowly down the wide aisle leading to the deep interior of the cathedral. As we took our seats with hundreds of others, I realized that this day would be one in which earth pilgrims that Thomas had been leading for so long would be gathering in his honor from all over the world.

We were a mixed bunch: distinguished scholars, scientists, economists, environmentalists, religious leaders, pilgrims-in-exile from institutional forms, Berry family members, people from indigenous tribes and diverse cultures. All had been transformed in one way or another by Thomas Berry's life and work.

I reflected that if we were all given the task of creating a composite portrait of Thomas, we would discover that we all believed we knew the "true" Thomas Berry and we would all be right. Yet there would always be more to the mystery of his identity than could be contained in any closed definition. Thomas was always in the process of becoming in a universe that was always becoming. Even now in this cathedral on this day.

He had spoken of our lives as the simultaneous first and last notes of a melody played in a sequence through time, but also existing outside the sequence in an eternal dimension. Today in this venerated cathedral, we who had come to this stopping place on this September day were being given the gift of remembering anew the eternal dimension within this man, within ourselves, within the earth of which he had made us more deeply aware, and within the universe of which we were all a part.

While waiting for the rituals to begin, I looked up at the magnificence of the vaulted ceilings above me and remembered the way Thomas' life had reflected both the simple and the magnificent—the simple in the way his physical presence lived with no concern for material things; his small monk-like room at Wellspring in his last years containing one narrow single bed, one bookcase with a few books and a dictionary left over from the gifting of his vast library to family and friends, one small cotton rug on the floor, and his leather recliner in front of the room's one window. His worldly possessions consisted of a few clothes, two pairs of shoes and a small table.

On the other hand, from his spiritual residence in the universe, Thomas constantly showed us its magnificence in all its "beauty, wonder and intimacy," from the "blazing stars at night" to "the miracle of dawn and sunset."

Though Thomas' physical legacy was inconsequential, his spiritual legacy was huge. Thus, this great cathedral was so appropriate for his service. The high vaulted ceilings reminded me also of our years at the Green Valley Grill in Greensboro where I tried to follow his thoughts as they soared up into the thermals.

Thomas Berry invited all who would come along with him into a vast and vibrant cosmos filled with great generativity and possibility. We were "great companions" who traveled with him back to the primordial Source of life itself and forward into a new century, companions he had awakened to the cosmic-human-earth process out of which new life might emerge for our time. Now on this day we had come together to honor him and the mysterious process that had brought us all together for this "auspicious occasion," as Thomas himself would have put it.

The music began and a procession of inspirited dancers emerged from all sides swirling and twirling silk windsock banners of fish throughout the cathedral, which brought a joyous celebration of the earth itself into the occasion. This was followed by readings, reflections and tributes from several of Thomas' great companions interwoven with evocative music from modern and ancient sources often accompanied by Paul Winter's hauntingly beautiful saxophone.

With each element of the service, I allowed myself to remember and reflect:

The excerpt from Tielhard de Chardin's *The Human Phenomenon* that Thomas had quoted to me at the TreeHouse years ago: "Seeing. One could say that the whole of life lies in seeing, if not ultimately, at least essentially. To be more is to be more united. ... But unity grows...only if it is supported by an increase in consciousness, of vision. That is probably why the history of the living world can be reduced to the elaboration of ever more perfect eyes at the heart of a cosmos where it is always possible to discern more."

I found myself deeply inspired and wrote these words on my program just as if I were in another conversation with Thomas: "All of life depends upon this seeing, this beholding with our hearts at the heart of the cosmos that can bring us into greater unity within ourselves and within the community of all living things."

Inwardly I heard him repeat what he had said so often, "We are being changed. We are being transformed to see everything in its true proportion. We are being driven down to the heart with its radical interior tendencies."

Thomas was leading us to shift from seeing with our conditioned mind to seeing with the heart and spirit. He was leading us down to our intuitive awareness connected like "a tendril to the heart of the universe" that allows transformation to occur.

Through a lifetime of study and contemplation in the service of the heart, Thomas Berry *saw* from an overarching sense of time that there is an implicate order of creation, a Mysterious Divine force bringing forth life. He *saw* the animating principle of soul in every living thing. He *saw* the infinite differences of all things within One universe that held them all "in a compassionate embrace."

Thomas *saw* Love as an inner presence to all things. He *saw* humanity at a crossroads and pointed to another way: a communion of all living forms in the universe, and a sense of the sacred. He taught that the presence of holiness lives in everything that lives, for holiness created life itself. Thomas Berry, taking the long view, *saw* a sacred universe holding all things, unifying all things, reestablishing what has been obscured through the centuries. In doing so he moved us out of the confines of our limited human community into an earth community and a universe community, opening new portals of thought for life to stream through, and showing us a way forward.

As the service continued, I began to feel something surfacing from deep within those gathered in the cathedral. There was something more happening that day as the readings went on from Thomas' own "Moment of Grace" interview, excerpts from his New Story, tributes and poems from those closest to him, all surrounded by magnificent original solo and choral music reflecting a love of the earth.

Gradually, as it seemed to me, from the deep layering of words and images and music that came forth to honor Thomas Berry on that September afternoon in the Cathedral of Saint John the Divine, a truth began to emerge of a Divine presence that had created all things through billions of years on earth that could move us past all dualities and into reconciliation with the universe, the earth and with one another.

In that *moment of grace,* all of us who were great companions of Thomas Berry were held in a *mutual presence* within a vision of an earth community in full communion. It was the vision Thomas had *held* his entire life and it was now being bequeathed to us for our collective transformation. In receiving it, we would be endowed with hope and new inspiration for the Great Work of our time. In receiving it we would recover a sense of the sacred.

Thomas had spoken of special, sacred *determinative moments* of transformation in which we celebrate our entry into life, maturity and the transition of death. It seemed to me that we who were gathered in the cathedral on that day were experiencing a determinative moment that would become part of the inner tissue of our lives and allow strength and creativity to flow into our future actions. It was a moment of grace and a moment of celebration, a moment of passing on into greater life for us all.

At the end of the service we stood and sang, "For the Beauty of the Earth." In the words of Tielhard de Chardin, we were "participants in a grand liturgy of the universe."

As I was leaving the cathedral, I remembered asking Thomas this question in his last days: "Thomas, how do you want the sacred story to go forward into the future?"

Without hesitation he answered: "It *is* going forward."

I didn't understand that at the time. Now I do.

And so does every creature, leaf, mountain and star.

Acknowledgements

One of Thomas Berry's favorite stories was about Reuben Snake, an Indian man who had done much for his tribe. When Reuben talked with someone about a monumental task of great importance that had to be undertaken, the other replied: "This is something awesome to try to do. There is only you and me. We must be very foolish to think of such a thing."

Reuben Snake answered in a rough voice, saying: "Yeah, but we'll find good companions along the way."

Thomas went on to say that in his own lifetime, he, too, had found good companions along the way, and "moment by moment the number has gathered until it is almost limitless."

In undertaking the writing of this little book, I have felt the awesome task of trying to bring Thomas Berry's wisdom and great humanity into these pages in a way that would reflect new forms of thinking and being in these days of great transition on earth and also reflect the ultimacy of the human spirit demonstrated by his life.

And, like Reuben Snake, I have found good companions along the way ...

First and foremost of these is my dearest soul-companion and partner, Scott Davis, who has urged me on to tell this story, patiently initiating me into the endless mysteries of technology, supporting me tirelessly through deep frustrations, and finally, devoting all of his spare time for a year to editing and designing all that must go into a finished work.

And then there is the remarkable contribution of Carole Chase, retired professor of religious studies at Elon University, who took the sixty-seven small notebooks and assorted paper napkins from my ten years of conversations with Thomas Berry and converted them into pages upon pages of word documents. Without her start-up help and companionship, this project would never have happened.

Then there are the dear friends who took on the thankless tasks of proofreading, while taking care to leave the content intact: Lou Wallace, Becky Story, Mark Spano and Chris Myers.

Additional good companions who knew and loved Thomas Berry also came forward in support: Thomas Rain Crowe, Tobin Hart, Rich Louv, Sr. Mary Southard, Drew Dellinger, Richard Lewis and Joanna Macy.

Special grateful acknowledgment needs to be made to Peggy Whalen-Levitt, Director of the Center for Education, Imagination and the Natural World, and Sandy Bisdee, Director of Children's Programs, both close companions of long standing, who have worked tirelessly to bring Thomas Berry's vision of "a new relationship between the inner life of the child and the beauty, wonder and intimacy of the universe" into the lives of children and teachers.

Finally, there has been the everlasting companionship of my little dog, Blossom, the deer in the orchard, the resident blue heron, the ponds with their swimming and croaking inhabitants, the mourning doves, finches, crows and cardinals, the loblolly pines, walnut and chestnut trees ... all of whom told me daily, "Tell them the story, the sacred story of the earth."

About the Author

Carolyn Toben is an educator, counselor and creator of new social forms with a spiritual dimension that foster cultural renewal. Her background includes degrees from the University of North Carolina Greensboro (Phi Beta Kappa), extensive postgraduate studies in spirituality, world religions, and depth psychology, and teaching in both secondary and college settings with an emphasis on alternative and interdisciplinary education.

In 2000, Carolyn founded what is now the Center for Education, Imagination and the Natural World, a work inspired by cultural historian and author, Thomas Berry, which offers children and teachers a new understanding of the human-earth relationship.

A grandmother of nine, she currently creates programs, retreats and events for individuals and groups seeking spiritual renewal and reconnection with the natural world at Timberlake Earth Sanctuary, her family-owned land in Whitsett, North Carolina.

For ten years, Carolyn spent many hours with the renowned priest, author and cultural historian, Thomas Berry, engaged in deep discussions about his foundational thinking on the human-earth-Divine relationship. *Recovering A Sense of the Sacred* is based on her personal notes, practices and reflections from these conversations.

To learn more about Timberlake Earth Sanctuary, visit timberlakeearthsanctuary.com.

Books by Thomas Berry

Buddhism
Hawthorn Books, 1967

Religions of India: Hinduism, Yoga, Buddhism
Bruce Publishing, 1971

The Dream of the Earth
Sierra Club Books, 1988

Befriending the Earth
Written with Thomas E. Clarke,
Stephen Dunn and Anne Lonergan
Twenty-Third Publications, 1991

The Universe Story
Written with Brian Swimme
HarperSanFrancisco, 1992

The Great Work: Our Way into the Future
Bell Tower, 1999

Evening Thoughts: Reflecting on the Earth as Sacred Community
Edited by Mary Evelyn Tucker
Sierra Club Books, 2006

The Sacred Universe: Earth, Spirituality,
and Religion in the Twenty-First Century
Edited by Mary Evelyn Tucker
Columbia University 2009

The Christian Future and the Fate of Earth
Edited by Mary Evelyn Tucker and John Grim
Orbis Books 2009